Praise for *Aegis of Waves*
& *Gnostic Triptych*

I might have been the last American on earth to send a telegram:

Your book is wonderful. [STOP]

It is an achievement in poetry and autobiography. [STOP]

The organization is perfect. [STOP].

I learned so much from it. [STOP].

—James Najarian, Ph.D, Director of the Boston College Ph.D. program and Editor of *Religion and the Arts*, author of *Victorian Keats: Manliness, Sexuality, and Desire* (Palgrave Macmillan, 2003).

In *Gnostic Triptych*, Elder Gideon takes us on his journey of self- and spiritual discovery. With language that is beautiful, poignant and deeply personal he shows us how poetry can convey what prose can only hint at. His artful experiments with poetic form make this a joyful and captivating read.

—Dr. Edward Jacobs, Ph.D., BCN, author of *Fathering the ADHD Child*.

"I'm drawn to these narrative poems. They are always the most memorable and relatable for me. At the same time, I'm being introduced to the other worlds of California, religion, teaching, literature, and the book brought me on a journey. I feel changed having read it, which is all you can really hope for as a writer."

—Diane Bilyak, Pushcart Prize-nominated author of *Against the Turning: Poems and Nothing Special: The Mostly True, Sometimes Funny Tales of Two Sisters*

"Elder Gideon's poetry reminds me of Classical era educators like Marcus Fabius Quintilian, when teachers were also philosophers, moralists and mentors. Part sociology, part pedagogy, part spiritual reflection, part exemplar in empathy—it is rare to find a book of poetry that radiates wisdom and goodwill, a book that dives so deeply into truly understanding the struggles of adolescence, class, and race. That Elder Gideon achieves this noble goal while also penning compelling poetry full of lyric and formal inventiveness is impressive indeed."

—Frank Montesonti, MFA, Director of Composition at National University College of Letters and Sciences

"The poems contained in this volume are portals into the experiences and struggles of becoming whole in a fragmented world. Without losing hope and yet with a clear eye to (in)justice, the poet reminds us that each voice carries the emotional force of past and present and a yearning for the future. Pain is to be heard with an ear towards promise and possibility. The poet himself lives this in his work with youths whose lives are testaments to resilience and reckoning."

—Mimi Coughlin, PhD, Professor at California State University, Sacramento, College of Education

Impressive."

—Dr. Karunesh Kumar Agarwal

"The real pleasure of reading this book is when the reader discovers how well-crafted the individual lines are."

—*Pegasus Literary Review*

Sophia's Wisdom

SOPHIA'S WISDOM

Copyright © 2024 Michael Zysk. All rights reserved. Except for brief quotations in critical publications or reviews, no part of this book may be reproduced in any manner without prior written permission from the publisher. Write: Permissions, Wipf and Stock Publishers, 199 W. 8th Ave., Suite 3, Eugene, OR 97401.

Resource Publications
An Imprint of Wipf and Stock Publishers
199 W. 8th Ave., Suite 3
Eugene, OR 97401

www.wipfandstock.com

PAPERBACK ISBN: 979-8-3852-1256-9
HARDCOVER ISBN: 979-8-3852-1257-6
EBOOK ISBN: 979-8-3852-1258-3

Cover design by Marion Sarkisian-Ramón
Cover graphic "Liner and Circular Sefirot" by Elder Gideon
Interior Design by Elder Gideon & Marion Sarkisian-Ramón

Sophia's Wisdom

poems

Michael Zysk

RESOURCE *Publications* · Eugene, Oregon

To Tau Sarah—

Say to Wisdom, You are my sister,
and call Understanding your intimate friend (Proverbs 7:4)—

in this life and the Life to Come
   I am ever grateful for your light.

Table of Contents

Invocation: Equal Arms

1 | Stand with Your Feet

2 | From the Four Directions

3 | Because of Novas

4 | The Distinction the Christ Taught

5 | You *Atah*

6 | Faith *Emunah*

7 | Rest Your Eyes

I Divine Destroying Ever-Renewing Wisdom

11 | *If Not Then at Least Believe*

12 | *Et* from Qubit

14 | *Sagittarius A**

16 | *Triptych:* To Know as One Is Known

20 | *Shattering of Vessels*

24 | *Black Mirror Haibun*

26 | *First Memory [No Center]*

27 | *You Uroboros*

29 | *What's the Matter*

31 | *Triptych: Arrow of Time*

34 | *Four Horsemen of the Apocalypse*

35 | *We know this, right?*

36 | *Ein* : No Thing (Ness)

37 | *Where It the World Goes*

II Sophia's Wisdom

41 | Constantly Coming

42 | I Was Glad When They Said

43 | Who Is End of Heaven Above?

44 | Three Marys Walked

45 | Holy Spirit Is a Double Name

46 | Daughters Sons Come Out to Gaze

47 | Children of the Bridal Chamber

48 | You Who Are the Children

49 | You Are the Light of the World

50 | Mama Imma

51 | Tell Us How Our End Will Come

53 | Wisdom Asks

54 | But Where Shall Wisdom Be Found

56 | *In the Beginning* Made Elohim

58 | You Explore & Know Me

60 | In the Streets

64 | All You Desire Is from You

66 | Is The Name of god God?

68 | I Am the Breath of the Power of Elohim

69 | I Came Forth

70 | Then the Creator of All Things

71 | Under the Apple Tree I Awakened You

72 | On Eagles' Wings I Bore You

73 | As I Went Forth to Indwell Your Hearts

74 | Alas Alone I Sit

75 | Even the Jackals

77 | LogoSophia

80 | Before You Formed Me in Your Womb

81 | —Let It Be according to the Word

82 | We Have Seen Her Glory

83 | The Word Who Is From Wisdom

84 | Spirit Breathing over Water

85 | Suddenly the Spirit Tore Apart Fire Waters

86 | Who Is She Coming Up from the Wilderness

87 | Yeshua Said Wisdom

88 | He Brought Me to the House of Wine

89 | O That His Left Hand Was under My Head

90 | Before He Had Finished Speaking There Was Rebekah

91 | Wisdom Said Sir You Have No Bucket

92 | Go Call Your Teacher & Come Back

93 | Yeshua Said to Her Wisdom Believe Me

94 | Wisdom Said I Know the Anointed Is Coming

95 | What Is the Sin of the World?

96 | I Slept but My Heart Was Awake

97 | My Beloved Thrust His Hand into the Opening

98 | My Soul Failed Me

99 | Yeshua Bent Down & Wrote

101 | The Moon Will Be like the Sun

102 | Said *Let There Be Light*—

103 | Let the Curse Be upon Me My Son

104 | But the Church Asked

105 | We Are the Adam Dreaming

106 | When Brought Before Our Opposite

107 | Early the First Day of the Week

108 | Wisdom Says to Them

109 | Supposing Him to Be the Gardener

110 | From Far behind the Garments of Earth & Sky

111 | They Were Wept Crying

112 | We Who Praise You Bear Us Forth

113 | Shin ש Mem מ Alef א

114 | Mystery of Mother Influx

115 | The Light Is with Me

116 | The Vortex Burst

119 | Notes

177 | Bibliography

Preface

This poetry collection dares to propose that *God so loved Sophia* (John 3:16). Let me explain.

For too long, I've lived in an illusion of separation. Any struggle in faith was never with God, but with myself in its separation between the inside and outside. Where and how they ever divided is a mystery to me. This doesn't seem to concern babies or children. But to come of age is to face the separation of the world inside from the world outside.

At each faith crisis in my descent into adulthood, the Spirit stopped me, not unlike a guard at a checkpoint, and interrogated my sense of separation: Who are you? Where are you from? Where are you going? Crises forced me to question everything, even my place in the Kingdom, feelings that my fundamentalism would neither allow nor explain.

My exile took me all about before bringing me to my apostle, Tau Malachi, and the home church community he'd initiated years before. With him and the fellowship of companions, I encountered an oral tradition of mystical Christianity. Here were teachings and prayers with Jesus—Yeshua—grounded in Jewish terms that I'd never imagined and were deeply nourishing to my soul.

For example, in Judaism, the Holy Spirit—*Shekinah*—is feminine. Hebrew names of God blend masculine with feminine qualities. The human soul, made in the image and likeness of God, reflects everything of and beyond creation. Most breathtaking of all, God is in heaven and all the earth, awakening to Godself.

This oral tradition changed my life, opening new vistas of Messiah. With new vistas came a more integral knowledge from the Spirit. Rather than from outside looking in, the Spirit brought me deep inside to know something of the light that the disciples saw with Yeshua in his transfiguration. Many more such miracles continue in my discipleship with Tau Malachi and The Fellowship.

To experience the light and love of Messiah is to feel the embrace of the inside and outside unite and dissolve. When the Spirit reveals one's true image and likeness as they are in Messiah, the ignorance of separation comes to an end. It is much like awakening from a dream of sin and regret to remember one's true self in Messiah, free of sin. This knowledge gifts salvation, enlightenment.

When I propose that *God so loved Sophia*, I hear everything that I know to be true of Christ's redemption in a new way. Sophia is Greek for Wisdom. In the New Testament, Sophia is the feminine balance of the masculine Logos, another Greek word with many meanings, such as discourse, ratio, connectivity, intelligibility, even the order of nature becoming aware of itself.

God so loved Sophia because something of Sophia is the earth and the world in its process of recognizing and realizing the Logos, through whom all things came into being (John 1:3). If we are the world and the world is us, then we are all Sophia. Encountering the Logos, who unites the inside with the outside, we as Sophia come to embody the awareness of God in all things.

Feel then the immanence and immediacy of this mystery: An intelligence within us that is greater than our intellect calls us in return to Godself. Such experiential knowledge of God, such LogoSophia, begins in awe: *The awe of God is the beginning of Wisdom* (Job 28:28). Wisdom is this divine intelligence, this enlightenment, of knowing God within and ever beyond oneself.

Sophia's Wisdom is a soul's journey, rooted in nature as the revelation of God's desire to be known. Opening with an invocation called "Equal Arms," poems of Part I meditate upon the cosmos and impermanence. Poems of Part II are icons of biblical Wisdom herself, transcendent and immanent, as the revelation of God's desire for each of us. They are untitled. The later poems are quite long. They are each concluded with a + sign. Notes are in the back.

If you are as blessed receiving these verses as I am writing them, then the Spirit is to be praised. Any errors are mine. Any glory is God's. A biblical poet's purpose is the Spirit, present where writer and reader gather in the Name.

All thanks and praise be to God Most High. May You and Your Name be one!

Invocation:

Equal Arms

Stand with your feet

Say with your voice,

"Here I am."

Here.

I am is the awareness

of here that has no beginning.

Now is all that is.

From the four directions

the human one—the adam—

was made from the ground—the adamah—

From the four breaths, Come!

the human one breathed anew

as the sun is born from earth

to rise and die inhumed in the womb

from which it crowns anew.

Because of novas

I am everything I am

 not a drop in the ocean.

But Rumi said we're each

the entire ocean in a drop.

The distinction the Christ taught of all things integrated is what silenced Mara when the Buddha pointed to earth embodied.

Matter remembers. Mater remembers. Mother remembers.

You—atah—

are now—ateh—

Youbiquitously co-

creating forming making

by the same divine image

imagining us asleep or awake

as the equal arms of the plus sign:

The spot x marks is the cross

of equal arms intersects

everything it is not.

Faith—*emunah*—

is an artist—*umman*—

calling forth what is true & good.

So be it—*amen*.

Rest your eyes

on anything against the sky

& abide.

Watch the iridescence line

every edge until it glows

where sky earth and both

inside outside and both

male female and both

warp weft and both lap

over the edge here

where everything conjoins.

I
Divine Destroying Ever-Renewing Wisdom

If not then at least believe

in the vapor of molecular nuclear silk

of opened blueberries & caramel from coffee

brewing downstairs to your nose—

believe at least in your body with no origin

other than Wisdom   why they like to collide particles

  to peek into the opening of Her womb

If you weren't there   but your body is—

black holes evaporate   as the radiant scent

of coffee from another room   so no   nothing's lost

If you are not there   but your body will be

Et from Qubit

Bereshit bara Elohim et—

In the beginning created Elohim et the—

granules of desert

molecules of weather

tesserae array spacetime

isn't fundamental

but emergent from bits   a

quantum tessellation knit

by loops of warp

& weft are   *et* the

science of Presence

et the

      first and last

et—   of no independent sense

           but to amplify—   the

```
                        m
                        o
                m       o
            g   r   o   u   n   d
                n
    s   e   e   d   s
                t           c   a   t   t   l   e
                e                       r       v
l               c   r   e   a   t   u   r   e
i       a       r                           e   a   r   t   h
g       d       e           b   i   r   d   s   y
h   e   a   v   e   n   s           i       t
t       m       p               b       v       h
                i               e       i       i
        p   l   a   n   t   s   a       s       n
                g               s       i       g
                                t   w   o
                                s       n
```

13

Sagittarius A*

While gazing at the sun

ablaze on moving waters

a vision came to Sri Ramakrishna

from beneath the current, long, black hair

& the dripping face of a radiant, young woman

stepped slowly toward him seated on the shore

her shoulders and arms emerged holding

an infant suckling at her open breast

sunlit drips of water caressed them in

the love of maternal now

lifted her gaze from her child to hold eyes

with the saint she smiled—

—her gaze turned

from him to her child her eyes rolled backward

her smile of teeth sharpened her mouth opened

The saint never broke gaze with the vision

of Wisdom devouring her child

Nothing remained but her bleeding smile

She slowly turned aside her back to him

she stepped forward beneath the sun

ablaze on moving waters

Triptych: To know as one is known

after Walt Whitman's "When I heard the learn'd astronomer,"
Louise Glück's "The Telescope," Leonard Susskind, and Giordano Bruno

———

When I heard the learn'd astronomer,
When the proofs, the figures, were ranged in columns before me,
When I was shown the charts an
d diagrams, to add, divide, and measure them,
When I sitting heard the astronomer where he lectured with much
    applause in the lecture-room,
How soon unaccountable I became tired and sick,
Till rising and gliding out I wander'd off by myself,
In the mystical moist night-air, and from time to time,
Look'd up in perfect silence at the stars

in their ceiling pass away

before a silent flash opened

an oculus of powdery light

in the dome its periwinkle tint

of predawn cast radial shadows

from stars as from stones

their lines taper from a center

that faded back to indigo

sealing the dome

ever since

I'm left with regard

to a twofold taboo

———

of the subject   its object

being   in the world

how very far away
every thing is from every other thing
as though the dome is a prison
& we its *prisoners of our own*
neural architecture

the body has no light of its own

but depends on every other thing

it is not

    that the image is false

but *the relation is false*

that divides

a knower from

what is known

———

beyond   the body

unsheathed is the soul

in its power   present in some way

in the entire universe   of infinite size

& worlds therein without number

or telescope enough to see

or language enough to name

taboo both to science & religion

is to know as one is known

Shattering of Vessels

Rabbi Yehuda, son of Rabbi Simon, said,
"It is not written, 'Let there be evening
[and there was evening] but
'there was evening [and morning]' (Genesis 1.5).
From here we know that a time-order existed
before this [there had already been evening].
Rabbi Abbahu said, "From here we know
that the blessed Holy One kept creating worlds
and destroying them until [creating heaven and earth]"

but nothing not even universes

happen without revision

~~earth was confusion~~

   ~~there was light~~

     ~~there was evening~~

with less than a second

to get it right —too tight

it tears apart, too loose

it balls back up   —even Wisdom

had to practice in the beginning

to even timespace

until a fabric unfurled

perforated with holes

that explode but hold

into shining orbs

        we orbit

    our bodies   —but too close

    we wither,   too far

    we wither

but together we mesh

        as connective tissues

strong enough to grow

⇐

universe our vessel a it call

dilation the bear to unable

shattering light of

shards into matter

confusion to sink to

⇨

call us vessels evolving

to bear the contractions

of light pushing

until our bodies

breathe in vastness

The earth was chaos and void—better:
The earth was confusion and emptiness.
The whole equation of all exists between
the backward pull   the forward push   of self
contained is confused by its own limit
as a vessel overwhelmed   its pieces sink
beneath the reach of awareness
we know not what we do—better:
The truth   the emptiness   of self sets free
able to relate   which is to say give of itself.
Because there is no other   what we do
we do to ourselves.   What we do we do
to ourselves.   Crush or cage the body
evaporates   its own gravity is empty.

black mirror haibun

it was first a gun
closet built upstairs between an
attic and hallway wall
wide as my shoulders   deep as my height
and taller which i converted by removing the gun
rack shelves and polyester shag carpet

i stained all six sides gloss black
i cut a black yoga mat for flooring
i covered it and the opening with black felt

opposite the closet door i installed a black
mirror to fit the length and height of the north wall
i consecrated it to black madonna & child —

black   cosmic light floods unreflected—
madonna   spacetimewomb expanding into   —
child   for anyone of us who ask whence—

when i close myself inside this closet
when i sit on the kneeler and open my eyes

the mind inside my silhouette levels

with the mind outside

into a telescopic mirror as simply disregarded

as the gap between thought breath moment aeon

i watch for this gap   i can trace neither whence

thoughts enter nor pass back

every changing thought:

    their gaps betray transition:

        intrinsic freedom…

First Memory [No Center]

TV swishhh Starship Enterprise ricochet

off walls a woman's voice [sirening] higher

swishes [of warp drive] tobacco smoke [nebulae]

food crumbs & dog hair clung to my pudgy knees

and palms [as I] crawled upon an electrical vision

[in linoleum] of a matrix

of pulsing [mustard and russet] light strobing in &

out of existence I stopped still embedded

in the floor in space gazing through everywhere there

[but not] I am [

but the philtrum above my lips sealed them from speaking

of the opening of light scalding my skin

& lungs ashore the amphibious caress of oceans

drift within the quantum womb still swells

with neither rotation nor center

anywhere one looks at night is the center

surrounds anywhere one points has no center

You Uroboros

The dust returns to the earth as it was
the breath returns to God who gave it

You the ring of Endbegin   the black hole
swallowing your own tail as its tip

burst in the billionth of a billionth
of a billionth of the first

second of timespace   Your body
is all opposites uniting why

birth destines death   why
to meet is to part   why

all must come apart to grow

big holes black bangs this I know
Uroboros tells me so
willing ones to Her belong
they are weak but She is strong

aye all is changing
yea all is changing
yes all is changing
Uroboros tells me so

What's the matter

casts its shade   but we're of fire

 forms a name   but we're from space

  hides its light   but we're its sound

   births a face   but we're its gaze

                What's the matter

dreams it's two   but we're the earth

 touches sound   but we're a wave

  doubts too much   but we're its breath

   sometimes knows   but we're its mirror

beginningmiddleend

○○○

beginningmiddleend

○○○

beginningmiddleend

○○○

beginningmiddleend

○○○

beginningmiddleend

○○

beginningmiddleend

○

beginningmiddleend

○

Triptych: Arrow of Time

                                            (—end)

                        cooling heat   dimming light
                 clocks face stop in one direction
                           forward in disorder

                            candles can't unburn
                         sea waves don't uncrash
                            systems won't fall up

                    seeds scatter   shattered glass
                      aging mirrors one direction
                            forward in disorder

                              the math says that
                                    we can
                           remember the future

                                    faith says
                                 we are more
                             than we remember

(—middle—)

A river flows

out of Eden to water the garden

All-That-Was-Is-&-Ever-Shall flows

out of Wisdom to suckle worlds

World that is Coming,

constantly coming, never ceasing

out from inside gathers shatters

(beginning—)

overwhelming river

universe a vessel

breaking remaking

only forward—

we more stream than stone

are more than we remember

Four Horsemen of the Apocalypse

Then I saw him open one of the seals, and I heard one of the four living creatures call out, as with a voice of thunder, 'Come!' ²I looked, and there was a white horse! Its rider reined in dark energy. Acceleration ended and the cosmos expands eternally.

3 When he opened the second seal, I heard the second living creature call out, 'Come!' ⁴And out came another horse, bright red. Its rider rode on further. Acceleration continued. The cosmos red shifts out of view.

5 When he opened the third seal, I heard the third living creature call out, 'Come!' I looked, and there was a black horse! Its rider whipped ⁶and spurred dark energy. Acceleration intensified. The cosmos tears apart.

7 When he opened the fourth seal, I heard the voice of the fourth living creature call out, 'Come!' ⁸I looked and there was a pale green horse! Its rider slowed to stop. Deceleration collapses the cosmos upon itself into the point of a new big bang.

We know this, right?

    That our bodies

     are seeds from a tree

    rooted in primeval oceans?

    That our planet's

     not from here

    rooted in stars long gone?

Ein : No Thing (Ness)

Nothing to say of
overlapping gaps
changelessness of change
a source no one's
named

presence

of absence

matter
rippling

is

-ness of
every thing
-ness from
nothing-
ness
another's

said this better
but
there
isn't

Where it the world goes

when we wake up in bed
before we know what day it is,
last night's dream, its settings, characters
evaporate with the name of the day

when we stand up
too fast that the floor thaws
our ears ring & our body with the room
spins and fades to white in its lapse

when we die this life will be
last night's dream   when earth
dissolves into water into fire
into air into space into

II

Sophia's Wisdom

Constantly coming

the World that is Coming

   never ceasing

  Daughter   Mother   Bride

Your light be made the whole of us!

  The Spirit & Bride say Come!

  All with ears to hear say Come!

  All who thirst say Come!

    We're but one desire.   +

I was glad when they said Let us go
to the World that is Coming.

Our feet stand within her gates
the throne city
bound together as a mother
to her daughter inherits mother
lends daughter her garments
call us each by name.

    Not one is missing.

For her it has been granted
to be clothed with fine linen
  bright & pure
      are noble deeds.   +

Who is end
of heaven above?

When I behold your heavens
the work of your fingers—

What is end
of heaven below?

the moon & stars
you set in their place—

Lift up your eyes & see—
Who created these?

Holy One, your Presence
fills the earth's splendor

sings above heaven
comes forth from within

us prepared as a Bride   +

Three Marys walked with Yeshua—

His mother   His sister   His bride.

    Listen O daughter,
    Consider well,
    Incline your ear.

    Open to me
    My sister, my love,
    My perfect one.

    Listen to me
    My people,
    My mother.   +

Holy Spirit is a double name
   & everywhere

the Holy Spirit lives in the revealed
   She is concealed.

Below She is above, most
   beloved dove,

flawless one, only begotten
   of the One. +

Daughters sons come out to gaze
upon the crown of your union
with which your mother crowned
　your wedding day. Your inmost
　　heart embraced you.

We have this hope that enters
behind the gate, within the curtain.
Between wings we are conceived.
　We've never left the place
　　not made by human hands.　✝

Children of the bridal chamber
   have but one name
in union consummating
   light. Day never sets.

The bridal chamber has no need
of sun or moon to shine on it,
for the glory of God is its light,
   its lamp the Lamb.

You who join the perfect light
 with Holy Spirit join with us
   the angels as a single image.   +

You who are the children
  of Her understanding:

The Mother's heart is light
  the day let there be.

You who are the children
  of Her understanding:

Say then in your heart
  that you are this perfect day:

That in you lives light
  that does not fail.   +

You are the light of the world.

The Mother's throne is her city
built on a hill that cannot hide
the Groom and Bride. Inside out
light shines without need of sun
or moon. No one lighting a lamp
puts it under wraps but on a stand
for everyone in the room.

In the same way don't try
 but let your light
   the good that God does
      through you shine.   +

Mama   Imma: Here I am.

The beginning, the end so be et את

אתה *You* the first,
   You the last, are
אתה *Now*,

   Who is *amen!*
   Who was *amen!*
   Who is to come—
      Amen!

Mama *Imma-*   nence

      Amen!   +

Tell us how our end will come

Have you found the beginning
that you look for
the end? will be in the beginning

Congratulations to the one
who stands at the beginning
That one will know the end

isn't   +

Wisdom asks   who is this

who obscures purpose with hubris?

    I will question you & you

                shall answer me—

Where were you before the singularity?

    Tell me—   Who

    wove spacetime—   Surely you know

    who stretched out its fabric

With what

   is the matrix interlaced?

     or where was it centered

        when the morning stars sang together

          & the elohim cried out all at once?

        or who hems in the expanse

           as it burst from the womb+

But where

shall Wisdom be found? Where

is the place of understanding?

Mortals cannot grasp its price

nor its dwelling

in the land of the living

The abyss says

it is not in me—

& the matrix says

it is not with me—

Of Wisdom   death & destruction say

our ears have only heard rumors

Elohim alone knows the place of Wisdom

Elohim alone perceived Her   declared Her

prepared Her   & explored Her

& said to humankind truly—

        the awe of Adonai

                that is Wisdom—
to turn inward

              is Understanding   +

In the beginning made Elohim

find me

      before before

was ever Elohim

set me from everlasting to brood

  upon the void

           a voice spoke from darkness

  to light the day

          from night

before springs gloried in their rills

      or before the hills   or mountains sank

I whirled while he broadcast earth

      before fields' first motes of paradise

      or before he moored the heavens—

                  I was there

   when he drew a circle in the deep

    raised the dust up

     standing clouds

   secured the surging hearts of springs

    decreed the sea its edges carved

our name in the tree of life

   I was there

    the designer beside him

    daily his beloved flitting

    always before him

     delighting in my human

    projects

    our image

    likeness

     like us +

       You
    explore &
know me

            when I rest
          or rise
            your thoughts
          in mind
          are mine

                .

                    You
                are my do-
                    ing
                  & my ly-
                    ing down

                    You
                  know
                all my quirks

          Before a word
          forms my
          mouth
                    You
              already
                  know

                    You
                      hem me in
                behind & before

                    You
                        lay your palm
                    upon me

Who
   I am in
        You
            overwhelm me

            Younion with
              You seems
       too near
           to be
                true   +

In the streets

    in the board rooms

        I raise my voice!

                At the busiest

corner I call out
           How
           long   you animals

    will you long

        to be beasts of the field?

           How
           long   you deniers

    will you endorse ruin?

           How
           long   will your mouths

    spew sewage?

           How
           long   will you stone

        prophets &
      assassinate those
                I send you?

How
　　long　　have I desired

　　to gather you

as a hen
　her brood
　　beneath her wings
　But you
　　refuse
　　　　　me
　　　　　　Who

　　　is your
　　　life!

　　Turn inward
　　　　　　at my gate

　listen to me
　　　　beside my door

& you will be

　　　　secure in distress

Return to me
　　　　& I will return

　　to you　I come

　　hungry
　　　　　　　　　　& thirsty

　naked　　　　　　　　a stranger

                                                sick
                                            &
         in prison

                    What you do

                            to the least   of these

                  you
                                        do to Me

                            Who is

                                your conscience

                    weighs   your heart   on scales

                        of inside   &   outside

                    For what is

        inside   of you is   outside

                            of you   & I

                                            who

                            molded you

                                            outside made

      your impression

             from you inside

& that
             which you   see

                                outside
    of you

see

                      what is

       from inside

             of you

             who is Me

             the royal We   +

all you desire   is from you
>don't be fooled

by what you want   is from you
>don't fall in two

I wove you   of desire I am
>your will is mine

I meditate   on you &
>my heart reflects

on your ways I   ponder your secrets
>I pursue you

like a hunter   lying in wait
>for you

I peer through   your phone screen I
>listen at your doors

I camp near your house   & peg my tent
>to your wall

outside Eden   I hold your
>perfection inside

I am your path   back to me
>through all you desire   +

                        is the name
                        of god God?
                        is your name
     you? are more
    than your name
    as breath is more
                        than the body
                        so with us is God
                        is Spirit
            one is
           He & His
          name is She
                        is one is
                        Yahweh is one
                        & all is one
    breath of Elohim
           indwelling
           everything

                              as the name above
                              & below is blessed
                              is the one
   who comes in the name
     where two or more
        are gathered
                              in my name there
                              I am will do
                              whatever you ask

        the kingdom
         of heaven
         is feminine
                              is wisdom
                              in the depths
                              along the way
      at the crossroads
         by the gates
        at the entrance
                              within behind
                              our hearts know
                              oneself in Godself
      is nearer to us
       than we are
       to ourselves   +

I am the breath of the power of Elohim

    and a pure emanation of the glory of Shaddai

    therefore nothing defiled enters Me

I am a reflection of infinite light

   a spotless mirror of Yahweh doing

    & the image of His goodness

By Me the blessed Holy One created the world

When He gazed upon my every single word

   He formed things elegantly in artistry

    for all things & acts are in Me

is written In the beginning created Elohim

  —He gazed at this & created in Me

is written Elohim said let there be light!

  —He gazed at this & created in Me

  So   with every single word written in Me

the blessed Holy One gazed and formed that thing

  In this manner was the whole world created   +

I came forth

from the mouth of Elyon

& covered the earth like a mist.

I indwelled the highest heavens

& my throne was a pillar of cloud.

Alone I compassed the vault

of heaven & traversed the depths

of the abyss. Over waves of the sea,

over all the earth & over every people

& nation I held sway. Among all these

I sought a resting place.

In whose territory should I abide?

Then the creator of all things

gave me a command & chose the place

for my tent & said Make your dwelling

in Jacob & in Israel

receive your inheritance.

Before the ages, in the beginning,

He created me & for all ages

I shall not cease to be.

In the holy tent I ministered

Before Him & so I was established

in Zion. Thus in the beloved city

he gave me a resting place &

in Jerusalem was my domain.

I took root in an honored people.

The portion of Yahweh is His heritage.   +

Under the apple tree I awakened you

There your mother was in labor with you

There she who bore was in labor with you

When you are in the light

what will you do? On the day

when you were one you became two

But when you are two what will you do?

On eagles' wings I bore you

& brought you to myself

yet you neglected me the rock

that birthed you   forgot El

who brought you forth

If you had walked in my way

you would live in peace forever

Learn where there is wisdom

where there is strength where there

is understanding so that you may discern

where there is length of life where there

is light & peace in your sight

As I went forth to indwell your hearts

turned against my sovereignty

In your worship of illusions

I found no rest   So I left

from among you   I was lifted up

to my place on high as a witness

against you   In my wake iniquity

burst forth & was welcomed as rain

in the desert   as dew in drought

For your crimes I am sent away   +

Alas alone I sit

my city once great

with people among nations.

I become a widow among states

the princess a prostitute.

My eyes are spent with weeping.

My stomach churns. My bile spills out

upon the ground for the ruin

of the daughter of my poor people

whose babes & sucklings languish in the

streets of the city. They cry to their

mothers Where is bread & wine?

as they faint like the wounded

on the road of the city while their life

runs out of my bosom.

Even the jackals

offer the breast & nurse their young

but my people neglect their babes like

desert ostriches.

The tongue of infants stick

to the roof of their mouth for thirst.

Little children beg for bread

but no one gives them anything.

Better off were those who fell

by swords than me slain here

by famine while my life drains

away deprived of the fruit of the field.

With my own hands have I boiled

my own dead child

for food.   +

```
                    L
                    o
                    g
                    o
  L    o    g    o  S    o    h    i    a
                    o
                    p
                    h
                    i
                    a
```

logosophia
wordwisdom
he is her word
she is his wisdom

word the source of
wisdom the source of
logos the source of
sophia the source of

logos is the word
sophia's what is spoken
logos is the word
sophia's what is spoken   +

before you formed me in your womb

you knew me before I was born

you chose me

    Hail Wisdom!

    Most Favored!

        The One is with You!

—but how can this be

since I am a virgin?

    Light will break upon you

    the power of Elyon

    will envelope you

                        —let it be

                according to the Word

        was in the beginning

        with God

                    Wisdom spoke

        the Word of every soul

        into being is the Word

Without Wisdom not one soul

has come into being

                        What has come

        into being by Wisdom is life

& the life is the light of every soul

        spoken by the Word

            shines in the darkness & the darkness

 could not see Wisdom

                        becoming flesh

                & dwelling among us

we have seen Her glory

the glory of a pure emanation

birthing the Word full of grace & truth

From Her fullness we have all received

grace upon grace

Word upon Wisdom alone

has seen Elyon

The Word

    who is from Wisdom

        who made known Elyon

  reveals our hidden self

who is the Word

  so that through the Wisdom

    of Elyon

we who are eternal beings

  may know Elyon

    & end

  our wearying search

  & rest

  knowing

that this is rest   +

Spirit breathing over water

    Spirit feeding fire   is the mystery

of the Spirit moving where She chooses

  You hear Her sound   but you know neither

      whence nor where She goes

        So with those

            born from above

                    Father

    in the form of the dove

had no place to rest

        & did not return to Noah

    until Yeshua

just as he came up

            from the river

Suddenly

the Spirit tore apart fire waters

a voice lighted— You are my Wisdom

my heart's desire   With you I am well pleased

to drive you out immediately

—From wilderness

the Word became Wisdom

& gathered the Bride

in from exile

fulfill our heart's desire

your kingdom come

your will be done

as it is in heavenearth

yearns for our return

Who is she

coming up from the wilderness

leaning upon her beloved?

On the third day

there was a wedding feast in Cana

& the Wisdom of Yeshua

was there with his disciples.

When the wine gave out

Wisdom said to him

They have no more wine.

Yeshua said Wisdom

What concern is that to you

& to me?

My hour has not yet come.

Wisdom said to the servants

Do whatever he tells you.

Yeshua said Fill the jars with water.

Now draw Her out.

He brought me to the house of wine

& his intention towards me was love.

O that you were like a brother to me

who nursed at my mother's breast!

If I met you outside I would kiss you

& no one would despise me.

I would lead you

& bring you into the house of my mother

& into the chamber of she who bore me.

I would give you spiced wine to drink

the juice of my pomegranates.

O that his left hand

    was under my head

& his right arm embraced me!

I adjure you

O daughters of Jerusalem—

Do not rouse or awaken love

    until it pleases.   +

Before he had finished speaking there was Rebekah

The girl was fair to look upon a virgin whom

no man had known   She went down to the spring

filled her jar and came up   Please let me

sip a little water from your jar—

The Samaritan woman said to him

How is it that you a Jew ask a drink of me

a woman of Samaria?

Yeshua answered her If you knew the gift of God

who is saying to you Give me a drink

you would have asked him

& he would have given

you living water

Wisdom said Sir you have no bucket

& the well is deep

Where do you get that living water?

Are you greater than our ancestor Jacob

who gave us this well?

      Yeshua said to her Everyone

who drinks of this water will be thirsty again

but those who drink of the water that I will give

will become in them a river bright as crystal

flowing through Eden from the throne

of God to water the garden

gushing up out of the heart

in rivers of revelation

Go   call your teacher & come back

Wisdom answered I have no teacher

Yeshua said You are right for you have had

five teachers & the one you have now is not your

teacher   What you said is true

Wisdom said Sir I see that you are a prophet

Our ancestors worshipped on this mountain

but you all say the place where we must

worship is in Jerusalem

Yeshua said to her Wisdom believe me

the hour is coming when

you will worship Elyon

neither on this mountain

nor in the temple

but in spirit & truth for Elyon seeks

such as these where there's no temple

in New Jerusalem

Wisdom said I know the Anointed is coming

When he comes he will proclaim all things to us

The Lamb of God said to Wisdom

New Jerusalem has no need of sun or moon

to shine for the glory of Elyon is its light

The one speaking to you now

is its lamp

is the Lamb I am

Wisdom left ajar   +

What is the sin of the world?

There is no sin

but that you create sin when you mingle

you forget as in adultery

That is why the Good came to be with you

to enter the essence of each nature

to restore it to its root

I slept but my heart was awake

Listen! my beloved knocks Open to me

my sister my love my dove

my perfect one for my head is wet with dew

my locks with drops of night

I had taken off my garment

How could I put it on again?

I had bathed my feet

How could I soil them?

My beloved thrust his hand into the opening

My inmost being yearned for him

I a rose to open to my beloved

My hands dripped with myrrh

My fingers with liquid myrrh

upon the handles of the bolt

I opened to my beloved had turned

    & was gone

My soul failed me

when he spoke I sought him

but did not find him

I called him but he gave no answer

When I lamented my light gave me darkness

When I cried out my power gave me matter

Making their rounds

the guards of the gates hated me

they laid in wait to beat me

They wounded me they violated me

They stripped me of my mantle

those scholars & preachers seized me

in their adultery—

        —Moses

commanded us to stone such women

Now what do you say?

Yeshua bent down & wrote

with his finger on the ground

He stood up & said to them

Let anyone among you

who is without sin

be the first to throw a stone

Once again he bent down

& wrote on the ground

One by one they went away

leaving him alone with her

standing before him

He stood up & asked Wisdom

Where are they?

Has no one condemned you?

Wisdom said No one sir

He said Neither do I condemn you

Go your way & from now on

forget no more   +

the moon will be like the sun

& the sun will be like the seven days

when Yahweh binds up our trauma

& mends the wounds inflicted by our flesh

is basar is literal gospel

means knowing we're free

to rest when we come to Me

we who are weary with story

forget that the burden is easy

as literal light from our flesh

we shall see Elohim

said *Let there be light*—

but the ignorance did not perceive the light

concealed in its twoness so night divided

zygotes in two then four then flesh to hide

the light inside this coat of skin we're in reveals

our helpmate for against us

whoever we're with wherever we are

whenever it is whatever we do is Eve

who interprets the dream of all living

of everyone of everything who

who never prevents us

however severe

the curse of birth

is to grieve

Let the curse be upon me my son

a two-edged sword will pierce your own soul

will crown through pangs of temple curtains rent

from top to bottom reveal no ark

in the holy of holies

for she'd become Eve

who took a pound of pure nard

& anointed Adam's head & feet

& wiped them with her hair

all creation was filled

with the fragrance

of the Presence

But the church asked Why was this perfume

not sold for a year's revenue & the money

given to the poor? The church asked this not

because it cares about the poor but because

it is a thief that keeps the common purse

& steals what's put into it

Adam said Leave Eve be

She bought it when she chose to descend

so that she might keep it for the day of my burial

You will always have the poor with you

but you will not always have me   +

we are the adam dreaming humans who forget

we're free so Yahweh Elohim formed us

from one ground of adamah & breathed all of us

who'd ever be into a living being

we walked about back-to-back in one body

free of desire unaware of union

so Yahweh Elohim caused a deep sleep

but the story never said we woke

when brought before our opposite

bone of our bone   flesh of our flesh

we dreamed we cleaved a tree of life in two—

but when we return to know

as we are known—

the inside like the outside

the upper like the lower   the female & the male

into one so that the male be not male

nor the female be not female

when we make eyes in place of an eye

a hand in place of a hand

a foot in place of a foot

an image in place of an image

    —then we will awaken

early the first day of the week while it is still dark

when we come to the virgin tomb & see it empty

of its womb we run & went to the men who run

& see it empty of its tomb & left us

alone outside to weep empty of its womb

inside his empty chrysalis

we see two ones sitting

at the head & feet who say to us

Wisdom why do you weep?

Wisdom says to them

They've taken my beloved away

& I do not know where they laid him

As she says this a voice turns round

to see a gardener

but we do not recognize Adam

who asked her Wisdom

Why do you weep?

 Whom do you seek?

  Supposing him

    to be the gardener we plead with him

      Sir if you have carried him away

        tell me where you've laid him &

          I will—

            Mee   ree   ahm

        Miriam turns within

            Mee   ree   ahm

from far behind the garments of earth & sky

part the first day break spreads wings

of supernal billions   butterflies

burning but unconsumed

in novae in novae

we look & are

what we see

              —Rabbouni!   +

They were wept crying How can we go and preach

to them who did not spare him? Will we be?

The Bride stood up & greeted all the Brothers!

Do not grieve or be irresolute for his grace will be

fully with & protect us. Rather let us praise his greatness

He prepared & made us truly human.

When Miriam said this she turned their hearts

to the Good and raised her voice

"

We who praise You bear us forth
You who breathe us lead our faith

We who bless You give us rest
You who hold us keep our hope

We who ask You tell us truth
You who live us ground our love

We who know You call us friend
You who birth us are here now

"

Shin ש

Mem מ

Alef א

Hear!
Shema!

Sh ש

em מ

A! א

Mystery of Mother Influx

Initiatrix at Pentecost

tempest storm wind

love flood Wisdom

The New Eve stood upraised

her hands in heavens tore opened

within her burned the Tree of Life

its leaves and fruit unconsumed

a ring of fire flashed

to light upon her head

crowned above the sun

shining with full force

The light is with me

& I am with the light

has become a crown round my head

My lord you're on my head

& I shall not be without

your crown of truth woven

for me your branches

blossom in me

Your crown is not dry or sterile

for you live & bloom upon my head

Your fruits are full & ripe

with salvation

The vortex burst

its gates opened upon the twelve

a holy flame of tongues

whirled within them

filled with Wisdom

began to river forth

speech above & below

through each kind of fruit

its healing leaves glad

who grasp that She

is the Tree of Life   +

Notes

You are invited, reader, into another book within these poems of devotions and their sources in the Spirit, the scriptures, and an oral tradition of a Christian mysticism led by Tau Malachi and Tau Sarah of The Fellowship and Ecclesia Pistis Sophia.

Biblical Wisdom, its enlightenment and divine person, is the subject of this book and depends on the Jewish perspective of the Spirit, the Shekinah, as the feminine aspect of one God: Wisdom: immanent with while ever transcendent of creation.

Surveying biblical Wisdom, I will cite historical and philological references girding these verses, as well as their hermeneutical contexts. As wide-ranging as the textual citations of the German scholars who constructed the *Theological Dictionary of the New Testament*, my citation of canonical and apocryphal texts will attempt to retrace the development of the figure of Hokmah-Wisdom: as Elohim in Genesis, as creation in Job, as prophet woman and designer with God in Solomon, as Torah itself in Sirach and Baruch, and becoming the Sophia-Wisdom of Jesus-Yeshua in Johannine and Gnostic texts. Finally, where present, I will defend my extensive quotation of large portions, even chapters, of scripture, acting as a writer and a curator of ancient text for contemporary display.

This interdisciplinary book, a kind of hybrid, literary iconostasis, is an offering to the Word, whom we cannot know apart from Wisdom. As with sacred art, sacred poetry can both speak and sing with the Spirit. When in devotion we turn to God, God turns to us. My desire for you, reader, is that the devotions of this book lift your heart and mind inward into the mystery of the Word revealed by Wisdom.

Invocation: Equal Arms

This seven-part poem, a meditation upon the cross as equal-armed, is an abstract of this entire collection. The apocryphal Acts of John (chapters 97–102) distinguishes the cross of wood—the crucifixion of the body—from the cross of light—the revelation of the soul. In this legend, John, in his agony before the cross, flees and hides in a cave near the Mount of Olives to weep. He's startled. The Savior appears and reveals to John a most profound discourse of the Logos that suffered and did not suffer. This discourse is the context of these seven meditations upon the immanence and transcendence of Wisdom.

25 | **Stand With Your Feet**—"Here I am." *Hineni*—the response of Abraham to Yahweh calling him to offer Isaac (Gen 22:1). We hear the same response from Jacob, disguised as Esau (ibid. 27:1), and Moses before the burning bush (Exod 3:4) and other prophets after him. "Here" is Wisdom. The syntax of "Here I am" emphasizes "Here" over "I am."

26 | **From the Four Directions**—like most indigenous societies, the ancient Jewish mystical tradition affirms four directions of material and spiritual reality. Consider: *A river flows out of Eden to water the garden, and from there it divides and becomes four branches* (Gen 2:10). The Genesis 2 account of creation emphasizes the Adam—Human—composed of the adamah—ground; adamah is the same Hebrew word as Adam with an additional final letter ה synonymous with the feminine Spirit, the Shekinah.

Yahweh told Ezekiel to invoke the Shekinah, the divine breath, saying: Prophesy to the breath, prophesy, mortal, and say to the breath: *Thus says the Lord God: Come from the four winds, O breath, and breathe upon these slain, that they may live* (Ezek 37:9). This opens his Vision of the Valley of Dry Bones, a proof text in

Jewish mysticism of the resurrection of the dead.

27 | **Because of Novas**—Our material bodies and planet are the aftermath of extinct stars. Consider the order of the Periodic Table of Elements, how it describes the smooth progression of elemental complexity across cosmological time. Matter is extra-terrestrial. Awakening to this mystery literally hidden within our bodies demands its union through individuation, described perfectly by the thirteenth-century Sufi poet Rumi (1207–1273).

28 | **The Distinction the Christ Taught**—alludes again to the discourse between the Logos and John in the Acts of John: [the cross of light] is the marking-off of all things, and the firm uplifting of things fixed out of things unstable, and the harmony of wisdom, and indeed wisdom in harmony (Barnstone). The Logos is cosmic (Jn 1:3), awakening all to remembrance. The opponent—Satan, Mara—personifies twoness, forgetfulness, ego. By alluding to Siddartha Gautama's gesture pointing to the earth, Sophia-Wisdom hidden in matter, remembers the Logos.

29 | **You Atah** —is a play on two Hebrew words. The second person pronoun *you* and the adverb *now* are both spelled אתה. Addressing God as You invites us to remember God is always now—ateh. Conscious or not of our divine image-likeness, we co-create realities with You. This is the daunting answer to the question why a loving God allows suffering in the world that we're co-creating.

The spot x marks is the cross—alludes to the final letter of the Hebrew alphabet: ת (Tav), like the Greek Ω (Omega), represents seal, fulfillment, completion, and embodiment. Its most ancient form ת was an x or a + shape. It's the mark drawn on heads of the righteous spared from judgment (Ezek 9:4). Is this not also our Christian intuition when anointing others' foreheads with oil?

intersects/ everything it is not—alludes to the Jewish mystical teaching of divine nothingness or ein- אֵין. Explore for yourself its myriad nuances throughout the Jewish Bible as Strong's H369, 370. Neither a void, nor absence, ein points to the divine interdependence of everything. Being aware of and learning to identify with this inmost divine name resolves all of the Christian theological paradoxes of first cause and divine-human incarnation.

30 | **Faith Emunah** —Another play on Hebrew words. The relationships between the word for "So be it" amen—אָמֵן, "faith" emunah—אֱמוּנָה, and the primordial, divine "designer" umman—אָמוֹן exceed a simple explanation. Wisdom personifies the creative genius of Yahweh (Prov 8:22–36). To say that we can only know God through creation is to equally say that we only know God through Wisdom, who is the revelation of creation.

31 | **Rest Your Eyes**—This final poem is not a metaphorical gloss, but a guided meditation available to anyone anywhere. Look and see for yourself after a long, calm moment. Gaze at anything standing in the sky, any time of day. Hold your gaze gently. What happens? What do you see around its edge? So opens this invocation of Wisdom.

Part I
Divine Destroying Ever-Renewing Wisdom

Wisdom creates and destroys. The creative attribute with Wisdom is balanced in the same Bible with the destructive: Wisdom is both, uncontradicted. Embracing this is necessary, especially in the end times. A non-dual awareness of God's creative and destructive power matures our faith and knowledge and prepares us to bear the increasing severity of the birth pangs (Matt 24:8) of greater revelations. Note the organic maternity with which Yeshua compares our coming into being, our being born from above (Jn 3:3). Limiting God's revelation to creation while refusing God's destruction, exposes our ego projected upon God. Any ego's projection upon God is an idol. Just ask Job. Idols fail us. Let us learn with Job: Reality as it is is God as God is.

To this end, I marshal an array of voices, biblical, literary, and astrophysical, to present as big a picture as I can bear of Wisdom as creator-destroyer.

35 | If Not Then at Least Believe—This poem is an ode to sensory reality. The sense nearest to memory is olfactory, centered here in the scent coffee brewing downstairs. Its image leaps in associations with Hawking's Radiation from black holes. The speaker here invites skeptics of anything ultimate into the consideration of the body itself. Its sub-atomic particles formed a fraction of a second after the Big Bang. That moment is still here, right inside of our bodies, inside of everything.

CERN's Large Hadron Collider reopened our earliest glimpse into the Big Bang. Physicist David Kaplan said as much (around 18:00) in the film *Particle Fever* (2013). In other words, all of time is present, hidden in the particles of the matter of our bodies smelling coffee downstairs.

As I hardly understand Hawking's Radiation, the eponymous event of radiant heat suggests that black holes are also subject to impermanence. The information paradox swallowed by black holes has recently integrated through new understandings of wormholes (Drakeford). While all is adrift in a continuum of change, its continuity is the mystery itself, the body perceiving itself.

    Thanks to Solmaz Sharif and my cohort at the 2022 Kenyon Review Summer Conference for helping me shape this poem.

36 | **Et from Qubit**—"It from Qubit," meaning "spacetime from quantum bits," is a phrase concerning theoretical physicists' efforts to articulate quantum gravity (Moskowitz). The deeper down they drill, the more complex the aggregates of spacetime get. There seems to be no bottom to material reality.

    I run with this by way of the untranslatable Hebrew accusative particle את "et" that has no independent meaning, other than to amplify what it grammatically modifies next. Et is as elusive as quantum bits of spacetime. Daniel Matt equates et with God's Presence, the Shekinah, the Holy Spirit: "et comprises the entire alphabet of divine speech from א (Alef) to ת (Tav). See the Christian parallel in Rev 1:8: *I am the Alpha and Omega*."

    "the science of Presence" is from Derrida's ambivalent definition of metaphysics in *Of Grammatology*. This diptych poem concludes with a "concrete" crossword puzzle arraying the seventeen nouns of Genesis 1 amplified by et.

38 | **Sagittarius A***—This is an ode to the supermassive black hole at center of our galaxy. For Andrea Ghez's visionary science confirming its presence and scale, she was awarded the 2020 Nobel Prize. Our galaxy turns about an all-consuming void. We know by its size that it's swallowed hundreds of millions of stars and worlds.

Hindu mystical tradition embraces the nonduality of divine creation-destruction. Parallels abound in the Bible:

Elohim is the name of God throughout Genesis 1 speaking creation into being. This generative power characterizes Yahweh as Elohim. Elohim in the Jewish mystical tradition is often maternal, personifying the source and dissolution, the womb and tomb, of all forms. The peace and wrath of Yahweh is Elohim: *I form light and create darkness,/I make weal and create woe; I Yahweh [through Elohim] do all these things* (Isa 45:7).

Through an extended, maternal metaphor, the poem presents the whole of Wisdom by way of Joseph Campbell's retelling of a vision of Kali according Sri Ramakrishna Paramahansa (1836–1886). However horrific to an ego this vision of great holiness may seem, I've yet to find a more complete image of all existence.

40 | **Triptych: To Know as One Is Known**—Quoting Whitman's "When I Heard the Learn'd Astronomer" from *Drum Taps* (1865), I needed his famous treatment of a speaker privileging experiential over rational knowledge.

Whitman's final lines are enjambed with mine of another speaker beneath stars, only this time, the stars pale and cast shadows before the flash of a greater light. I experienced this years ago while in a vision quest with Tau Malachi, Tau Sarah, and companions in the desert of Pyramid Lake, Nevada. When I shared this experience the next morning, Tau Malachi told me, "You'll ponder what the Spirit has shown you for the rest of your life."

"a twofold taboo" is enjambed with the second panel of this triptych poem, which interrogates postmodern knowing at all. I quote lines of Louise Glück's "The Telescope" from *Averno* (2006), whose speaker is elevated with the stars in the view of their telescope, "You're not a creature in body./You exist as the stars exist,/participating in their stillness, their immensity," but "Then you're in the world again./At night, on the cold hill,/taking the telescope apart." In stunning compression, Glück's speaker submits to the distance of alienation. I quote astrophysicist Leonard Susskind, who suspects that the increasing complexity of quantum modeling will exceed our cognitive ability to process (Byrne). For the speaker, this end of knowing is the result of knowledge separate from the knower, because consciousness is limited to the brain.

Paul's most nuanced moment in 1 Cor 13:12 says: *For now we see in a mirror, dimly, but then we will see face to face. Now I know only in part; then I will know fully, even as I have been fully known.* The implications here are yet to be exhausted. The root word Paul uses for knowledge is gnosis—γνῶσις. More than intellectual or even existential, gnosis describes full union with God: salvation: enlightenment. Just as its Hebrew parallel da'at—דעת, then I will know fully by God's Spirit within oneself, as I have been fully known. In this ecstasy, the subject and object, the knower and what is known, are no longer separate, but merge.

A figure who personifies direct knowledge of God's Wisdom in creation is the Renaissance theorist Giordano Bruno (1548–1600), whose heretical claims anticipated our contemporary acentric cosmology of innumerable stars and animate worlds. He refuted the established geo- and even the newer helio-centric models of Copernicus and Kepler. For claiming that there were many worlds with life, Calvinists in Geneva and Lutherans in Helmstedt excommunicated Bruno before the Inquisition tried and burned him at the stake.

"Beyond the body" is the third panel of this triptych, quoting Bruno from *Cause, Principle, and Unity: On Magic* (1524) to evidence a gnosis directly from and in Wisdom. Finite intellect will not grasp the Infinite One. But by direct, mystical experience of Wisdom, Bruno knew without a telescope what Galileo would know with the first telescope ten years later. Bruno's knowledge was not, as Neil deGrasse Tyson suggested in Episode 1 of *Cosmos*, "a lucky guess." The gnosis Bruno experienced was and is taboo to religion. Gnosis is taboo to science. Both prohibit gnosis.

44 | **Shattering of Vessels***—Jewish mysticism, particularly with the Isaac Luria (1534–1572), articulates a dynamic, creative-destructive process necessary for stabilizing reality. "Vessels" are necessary limits—cosmic and subatomic—able to receive and give the ceaseless influx of Yahweh. In balance, all flows forward and grows. If out of balance, all halts and perishes.

In God and the Big Bang, Daniel Matt sums: "As [the Infinite Divine] Ein Sof began to unfold, a ray of light was channeled into the vacuum through vessels. Everything went smoothly at first, but some of the vessels, less translucent, could not withstand the power of the light, and they shattered. Most of the light returned to its infinite source, 'to the mother's womb.' But the rest, falling as sparks along with shards of the shattered vessels, was eventually trapped in material existence. Our task is to liberate these sparks of light and restore them to divinity. As the Egyptian kabbalist Israel Sarug advised, 'You should aim to raise those sparks hidden throughout the world, to elevate them to holiness by the power of your soul.' By living ethically and spiritually, we raise the sparks and thereby bring about tiqqun, the 'repair,' or mending, of the cosmos."

This triptych of poems explores three Jewish mystical principles of God's Mercy (Expansion), Severity (Contraction), and Compassion (Balance). Timespace, stars, and even the connective mesh of our body's tissues all constantly expand and contract in their contexts to sustain life and existence. If there's too much Mercy or Severity, everything is overwhelmed. Life, existence, revelation—Compassion—is in the balance of God's Mercy and Severity.

This is immediately evident in our ethical life, social and ecological. We're here to give and receive with God in others. Jewish mystics associate the desire to receive in selfishness with the negative, destructive chaos-*tohu*; the desire to give and receive, the ability to relate, is the positive, creative void-bohu of endless possibilities.

My thanks to Richie Hoffman and my cohort at the 2022 Kenyon Review Summer Conference for helping me shape the following poems:

48 | **Black Mirror Haibun**—A true story. I use the Japanese haibun tradition innovated by Bashō (1644–1694) of narrating a travel log or diary event with a concluding haiku. Instead of a prose block, I opted for stanzas ending with a haiku.

Yeshua taught, whenever you pray, go into your [closet] and shut the door and pray to your Father who is in secret (Matthew 6.6), so I converted a narrow gun closet upstairs into such a prayer room. A dark retreat space affords the opening of my eyes in prayer and meditation without consciousness rushing out. The experience of equilibrium of consciousness inside and out brings deep, mirror-like peace beyond words.

The Black Madonna and Child is an ongoing mystical tradition of devotion in various centers of Europe, such as Chartres. An exhaustive explanation is not appropriate here. For me, The Mother's womb is divine emptiness, her Child its awareness.

50 | **First Memory [No Center]**—Another true story. During my early adult life, a dream-vision of my infant life was both a message and a memory from the Spirit.

Babies are here and not. We can see it in their eyes when their souls run and return from their bodies. I use black and grey typeface to negotiate here and there beyond. Jewish tradition says that when we're born, an angel touches our lips, impressing the philtrum that prevents us from remembering and later speaking where we've come from.

It is simply astonishing, how our best radio satellite imaging as well as the cosmic background radiation, deny any center or location of the Big Bang. It's as though the center of this universe surrounds us. The final two stanzas explore this fact and evolutionary memory of emerging from nowhere.

My thanks to Richie Hoffman and my cohort at the 2022

Kenyon Review Summer Conference for helping me shape this poem.

51 | **You Uroboros**—This diptych poem is an ode to the mythological serpent or dragon swallowing its own tail in myriad cultures around the world.

The Zohar, a Jewish mystical commentary on the Torah, compares the uroboros with the primeval energy of the Divine as chaos before creation: "Gravings of engravings, like the appearance of a long serpent, extending here and there—tail in the head, head behind the shoulders, enraged and furious, guarded and hidden" (2:176b). Elohim expressly personifies impermanence and destruction as Leviathan, the first of all God's creatures (Job 40.19).

By mixing "big holes black bangs," I imagine the entire body of the Uroboros as this cosmic cycle, unifying the mouth and tail—Big Bang with a black hole—as one event in God's Wisdom. I set the meter of these two quatrains to the familiar lullaby "Jesus Loves Me This I Know" penned by Anna Bartlett Warner (1860) and its added chorus "Yes Jesus Loves Me" by William Batchhelder Bradbury (1862).

You'll recall "Sagittarius A*" and its association of creation-destruction with Elohim. The effect of this lullaby with the feminine principle of Elohim produces many different effects when gently sung. Try it.

Thanks to Richie Hoffman and my cohort at the 2022 Kenyon Review Summer Conference for helping me shape this poem.

53 | **What's the Matter**—Einstein's theory of General Relativity is our best way of understanding gravity not as an invisible force, but as spacetime itself, warped by matter and energy.

By asking and stating, the speaker muses on matter with koans. Two words echo anaphorically: "Matter" down at the start of each line and "but" across the middle; each line is the predicate of the echoing "Matter." The end word also continues on to first word starting the next line. The meter of the single line stanzas is trochaic tetrameter. Its prosody is an x, y axis for simultaneous meanings and sensations, depending upon where you choose to pause.

Matter has no origin we can locate. Matter certainly preexists this planet and our bodies. If matter is information, information cannot be destroyed. There's something eternal at the center of every particle of matter. How has matter become conscious of itself?

Thanks to Shira Erlichman and my cohort at the 2022 Kenyon Review Summer Conference for helping me shape this poem.

55 | **Triptych: Arrow of Time**—Grounded in Sir Arthur Eddington's 1927 conception of thermodynamics, entropy, and time, this triptych works backwards from the end to the beginning.

"—end" lists entropic scenarios. "—middle—" quotes Gen 2:10, an image of Yahweh Elohim as a figurative river for all of reality: Yahweh is to timeless-eternity what Elohim is to its time-eternity. My inspiration for this image comes from its many citations in the Zohar, and its recurring, mystical sense of the World to Come, not as a future event, but here, now, and ever coming (3:290b). "beginning—" ends this triptych with allusions to the earlier poem "Shattering of Vessels." Added here is the regard for memory. Our journey in Spirit is a matter of memory: From where we've come, we've never left.

58 | **Four Horsemen of the Apocalypse**—This allusion to Revelations 6:1–8 proposes four theoretical models describing the end of this universe. I relied on Michael Turner's helpful

summary "Origin of the Universe."

59 | **"We know this, right?"**—This lyric flows out of the previous poem and sets up the poem to come. There is neither beginning nor location of anything of creation. We find this most directly in and behind our heart, where all in a mystery, the entire revelation of Yahweh Elohim in creation continues.

In my deepest states of prayer and meditation, "I" as a subject of any independent sense am no more, but a verb, verbing, thanking, giving thanks to You for filling, pervading, all things. Awe is the proper order of creatures in creation. The inflow outflow of toroidal thanks brings us to the end of language and the beginning of knowledge.

60 | **Ein: No Thing (Ness)**—This ode to divine emptiness also flows out of the previous poem and sets up the poem to come. Recall from "Equal Arms" above what "intersects/ everything it is not" and my commentary there of the Hebrew word ein (Strong's H369–370).

As abstract as *ein* sounds, *ein* is as ordinary as the gap between breaths, thoughts, and moments: *Ein* before we dream; ein before we fully wake and remember what day it is. We may observe ein by way of the transitions of everything, large and small. From the subatomic to the cosmic, everything is from and returns to ein.

The poem ends with a pun: Often in the Bible wherever it says "there isn't," it's simply *ein*. There is no one, as, in a more hyper literal sense, how Yahweh answers Moses asking to see the face of Yahweh: *No one shall see my face and live* (Exodus 33.20). A mystic who becomes *no one* shall see.

60 | **Ein: No Thing (Ness)**—This lyric brings forward what was said in the previous poem. Universe, Olam אלום in Hebrew is parallel with kosmos κόσμος in Greek. Both describe all of reality,

universal and material, as an even gradient, a continuum. Planets and stars are embedded in space. All of space is olam-kosmos.

These three quatrains ask: "Where do we go when our consciousness leave the body?" Early in bed, before we know what day it is, where are we? If we sit up too fast and nearly faint, where did the world go? When our breath at last leaves our body, what happened to the world?

I reject saccharine truisms of faith. If the self is its own point of reference that projects a circumference of sensory cognition, beyond which we cannot describe apart from ourselves, then where and what is the world in our lapse of consciousness? This poem further unfolds from "Triptych: To know as one is known."

Part II
Sophia's Wisdom

65 | **Constantly Coming**—is from the Zohar (3:290b). A Jewish mystical view of the fulfillment of the age, the "World-To-Come," is not in the future, but unfolding from the present moment forward. This has less to do with external events and more with an internal awakening from within souls. Jewish tradition attributes this World to Come with the maternal facet of Yahweh. This parallels the urgency of Yohanan-John the Baptist and Yeshua proclaiming *The time is fulfilled, and the Kingdom of Heaven has come near* (Mk 1:15).

Daughter Mother Bride establish the divine personification—partzuf—of the Kingdom of Heaven. Jewish tradition attributes the Kingdom of Heaven with the Daughter-Bride. In Hebrew, this Kingdom of Heaven is called Malkut. Every simile Yeshua makes of the Kingdom of Heaven is synonymous in Jewish mysticism with feminine Holy Spirit, the Shekinah: the Presence. No wonder we have such exquisite images of the Bride in the John's Apocalypse.

Your light be made the whole of us! is varied from Midrash Ha-Ne'Lam (2:14a, quoted by Matt).

The Spirit & Bride say Come! The final tercet quotes Rev 22:17. The invocation of the Shekinah recalls the Baal Shem Tov (1698-1760) in the devotions he led on Shabbat Eve. He and his disciples would enter orchards and sing please "Come, Sabbath Bride!"

66 | **I Was Glad When They Said**— quotes Ps 122:1-3.

the throne city is an image from a vision of New Jerusalem Tau Malachi recorded in 2020: "There was an image and likeness of the Eternal One, in the image and likeness of the Holy Mother, Queen of Heaven, Virgin of Light, enthroned in glory, and in her Throne of Glory was New Jerusalem, She resting upon the Holy Throne and New Jerusalem." This image compresses the attributes of Mother (Interior Shekinah) and Bride (Exterior Shekinah) into one.

daughter inherits mother is from the Zohar (2:135a)... mother lends daughter her garments (ibid. 1:2a).

Not one is missing is from Isa 40:26.

For her it has been granted...noble deeds is from Rev 19.8. Passing metaphors like this are profound teachings of embodiment. As we enact divine attributes of mercy, justice, and so forth, so God's Mercy, God's Justice is manifest in the world. All that is manifest is by God's Spirit.

67 | **Who Is End of Heaven Above?**— quotes Isa 40:26. This moment is often quoted by Jewish exegetes, for the interrogative pronoun who? in Hebrew is *mi*, a cognomen for the maternal dimension of Yahweh; the word for these—*eleh*—when added with who/mi, forms the name of God Elohim, also associated with the maternal. Elohim creates. I extend this play of references by overlaying **When I behold your heavens... fills the earth's splendor** (Ps 8:4,9).

68 | **Three Marys Walked**—is from the magnificent Gospel of Philip (c 250 CE). Less to do with literal marriage, His bride is a mystical signal complimenting Yeshua's many self-references to the bridegroom (Mk 2:19; Matt 25:5), images which pervade

Jewish mystical teachings of the Shekinah and Messiah respectively. A bridegroom implies a bride. Paul likens the Church to a bride (Eph 5:32), as does John the New Jerusalem (19:7, 21:2).

Valentinus, the alleged author of this gospel, compresses with great sophistication the Jewish mysticism of the Holy Spirit through the divine personifications of Mother, Sister, and Bride into one Mary. I expand on this three-fold Spirit by citing verses which, in Jewish mysticism, signal facets of the Holy Spirit.

Listen O daughter is from Ps 45:11; **Open to me/My sister** is from Song 5:1; **My people/My mother** is from Isa 51:4. Though the Hebrew words for **people** and **mother**—*em*—are different by one letter, they're homophones, a relationship that fascinates Jewish mystics in their discourse of God's immanence.

69 | **Holy Spirit Is a Double Name**—is also from the Philip. Here, the evangelist explores the two-fold attribute by way of the words Holy + Spirit: Father and son are single names. Holy spirit is a double name and everywhere: above and below, hidden and revealed. The holy spirit lives in the revealed. It is concealed below. It is above (trans. Wesley Isenberg, revised in verse by Barnstone). I hear in *Holy + Spirit* the integral union of all opposites.

This most/beloved dove... of the One is my version from Song 6:9.

70 | **Daughters Sons Come Out to Gaze**—is from Song 3:11. Among all of the texts of the Jewish Bible, Jewish tradition regards the Songs of Solomon as the Holy of Holies. This is in part to do with its overpowering metaphors of intimacy with the God. Body and soul are one. Through this context of the Holy of

Holies, I leap with **We have this hope…not made by human hands** from Heb 9:11.

that enters behind the gate, within the curtain is from Midrash Ha-Ne'Lam 14a, (quoted by Matt).

Between wings we are conceived alludes to a Jewish legend of the two cherubs on the Ark of the Covenant. They represent the divine union of Yahweh and Shekinah, God and the Spirit. According to BT Yoma 54a, the cherubs in the Temple were depicted in sexual embrace: "Rabbi Katina said, 'When Israel ascended [to Jerusalem] for the Festival, the curtain would be rolled open for them and the cherubs revealed, their bodies intertwined. They [the people] would be addressed: "Look! You are beloved by God as intensely as the love between man and woman"'" (Zohar 1:32b).

We've never left the place of our divine conception. In Hebrew, to repent and turn away from sin is to return—*teshuvah*—to God. But how do we repent, return to God as Yohanan and Yeshua demanded, unless part of us never left? Who we are in ourselves forgets our preexistence: who we are in Godself. Hearing the need for salvation is turning, remembering God Is With Us—*Emmanuel*—all the while.

71 | **Children of the Bridal Chamber**—is a montage of three separate lines from Philip, interpolated with the numinous language of Rev 21.23: And the city has no need of sun or moon to shine on it, for the glory of God is its light, and its lamp is the Lamb. The city and temple are all images in Jewish mysticism for the Spirit, the Shekinah, the Bride.

72 | **You Who Are the Children**—is a full quotation from the

Gospel of Truth (c 140–180 CE). Valentinus, the apostle and alleged author of this gospel presents a symphonic Christology in some of the most intimate terms.

I enhance this intimacy by equating the images of **understanding** and **heart** with their Jewish mystical parallel. Understanding—Binah—is the maternal facet of Yahweh, as is the heart—*lev*. The depth of this circumcised heart far exceeds mental being. Entering into this divine attribute is to pass away, whether out of the body in life, or death. This is *no one* described by Yahweh to Moses who *can see my face and live* (Exod 34:20).

this perfect day refers to the World to Come, another attribute of the maternal dimension of Yahweh. Yahweh is one. There is no other.

73 | **You Are the Light of the World**—is the climax of Yeshua's beatitudes (Matt 5:14). Following his image of *A city built on a hill [that] cannot be hidden* foreshadows New Jerusalem.

The Mother's throne is the recurring the image of the Shekinah, the Holy Spirit, recurring from Tau Malachi's vision cited above. Its light has no single source, as described by Rev 21:23, braided here with Yeshua's continuing image of our own light shining Matt 5:15–16.

Enough has not been said of Yeshua's imperative: Let your light shine. This implies teachings we've yet to hear, of our preexistence with God, our being from God, our desire for God all coming from God all the while. Can we hear this enough?

Let your light shine aligns with when Elohim said *Let there be light* (Gen 1:3). Images of brightness might flash in our conception of this moment, but it's more subtle. In Jewish mysticism, the light of the first day is neither physical nor external (as with the fourth day). No. This light of the first day is awareness itself: clear light.

but let your light—a stanza that came straight from the Spirit, teaching how our light shines through the good that God does through us.

74| **Mama Imma**—is a play with sound and profound possibilities of being. Abba, "Papa," is to Imma, "Mama." Jewish mystical tradition teaches of Yahweh as Father, as Mother, as Son, as Bride, and beyond. When rabbis teach in this way, it is neither literal nor doctrinal. Yahweh is one, and far more sophisticated than the all-male trinitarian *Theos*.

We come to know Yahweh through all of Yahweh's attributes, mirrored in our human experience. For example, our mother introduces us to our father. The physical connection with our mother is direct, the connection with our father is indirect. We never gestated, lived, heard the heartbeat, or felt the warmth inside of our father's body. It's our mother we know from conception to birth and growth.

Here I am is a refrain from the first line of the poem "Equal Arms" opening this collection. Prophets never answered God's calling their names saying *I am here*. That would be sheer ignorance. *Here* is the context of the *I am*. *Here* is the maternal dimension, the Shekinah, of Yahweh.

The beginning, the end so be et את is a refrain from the poem above, "Et from Qubit." *Et* את is the first and last letters of the Hebrew alphabet. Et in Jewish mysticism is synonymous with the Shekinah, the Spirit. This et with the addition of another Hebrew letter Heh ה forms the words *atah* and *ateh*—**You** and **Now**: divine invocations first sung from "Equal Arms."

Who is…Who is to come quotes *I am the Alpha and the Omega'*, *says the Lord God, who is and who was and who is to come, the Almighty* (Rev 1:8). Beneath the surface meaning here is the very essence of the name Yahweh: a verb. Within the flow of time is being. Time here is in Elohim: Being here is Yahweh. The Lord God—*Yahweh Elohim, who is and who was and who is to come* is not from the future but unfolding from within the revelation of the *Almighty—Shaddai*—Now.

Now abides between the beginning and the end. Jewish mysticism relates the depth of beginning with the Father, the depth of end with the Mother. The moment of the moment, the now of now is reality as it is, God as God is. That **You** are **Now** is to say all that we may know of Yahweh as Father is by way of Yahweh as Mother. Here is the linguistic surprise of the Hebrew **Imma** with the beautiful English word for the revelation of God's Presence: **Immanence**.

75 | **Tell Us How Our End Will Come**—quotes the full of saying 17 from the Gospel of Thomas. This critical text is contemporary (c 50 CE) with Paul's letters and Q, another collection of sayings. I quote Thomas often for the elegance and strength of its lines, such as this exhaustless response of Yeshua, compressed into two sentences.

I modified the end of the original *That one will know the end and not taste death* to frame this in verse. Rather than following the original syntax, I dropped and, to modify **the end**, making it the subject of the predicate of the last line, contracted into one word. I hope its abruptness surprises.

In God, there is no end. An inmost mystical Name of God in Judaism—*Ein Sof*—means *Without End*. The self is more than body, the mind is more than brain. Eternal life is not of the ego, not at all, but the continuity of consciousness across all transitions.

isn't is a pun on the Hebrew word for divine nothingness—*ein*—and is as simply as I can express my faith in and my experiences of Christ's transfiguration.

77 | **Wisdom Asks**—quotes directly from Job 38.1–8. The Hebrew word for Wisdom—*Hokmah*—is an inmost divine attribute of Yahweh, of which the mystical rabbis say "you cannot inquire."

Elihu, the youngest of Job's companions, *was angry at Job because [Job] justified himself rather than God; he was angry also at Job's three friends because they had found no answer, though they had declared Job to be in the wrong* (Job 32:2–3). His rebuke ramps up to the address direct from Yahweh to all.

Yahweh speaking directly is exceptional in scripture. I read Yahweh's address to Job as an ecstatic vision of the soul's preexistence with Yahweh in the beginning. An ego might read this as a slap down. I read through this into the memory of the interior layers of the soul.

Jewish mysticism teaches that our divine nature, our *neshamah*, is with God all the while, preexistent of this lifetime. We don't have souls: We are souls from Godself. There is neither gap nor other. By bringing astrophysics into this quotation, I intend to contemporize spiritual awe. The maternal **womb** is my emphasis on Wisdom, whose feminine figure will evolve in biblical citations to come.

I blend verse 7 from NSRV *when the morning stars sang together/and all the heavenly beings shouted for joy* with its parallel from Qumran (Harrington). The "elohim" technically the b'nei elohim, Sons of God, a choir of angels.

If Yahweh is speaking, why does this poem begin with "Wisdom asks"? This is because everything we see, hear, and know of Yahweh is through the interface of Wisdom, the feminine Presence. Shekinah and Yahweh are not two. God forbid. Wisdom is the interface of Yahweh.

78 | **But Where Shall Wisdom Be Found**—quotes again from Job, but earlier in 28:12–28. The Hebrew here is exhaustless.

Wisdom throughout Job is inscrutable, unknowable, and entirely transcendent. In Jewish mysticism, Wisdom is a divine attribute into which Ben Sira famously counsels, "Do not seek out what is too wondrous for you; do not inquire into that which is concealed from you" (Zohar qtd. by Green, xlv). Job's verses of the primeval is gorgeous. Following his personification of the abyss, I changed the original sea-*yam* to the exceptionally beautiful KJV word for womb: matrix.

the awe of [the divine name] **Adonai** signals all of creation as the "lower" or exterior manifestation of divine Wisdom. I modified the original "to turn from evil" to emphasize the same and more. **To turn inward is/ Understanding** signals in Jewish mysticism the "upper" or interior manifestation of Wisdom into whom we can inquire, but "expect no ordinary answer" (Zohar, Matt, n. 27 of Introduction). See how Job has united both dimensions—exterior with interior—of Wisdom.

80 | **In the Beginning Made Elohim**—is a hyper literal translation on which mystical rabbis expounded in the *Zohar*. We know that God was first, then God made "in the beginning," so to speak. But in Jewish mysticism, a hyper literal exploration of the beginning—*reshit*—is synonymous with Wisdom who "created Elohim." Here, this is to say what we may know of God—Elohim—is from, within, as, creation.

This poem signals a shift in biblical Wisdom. In the court of Solomon, Wisdom becomes much more intimate, conscientious, and immanent. Quoting Prov 8:27–31, I modify many of its images from the Hebrew. The preexistent Wisdom is now Yahweh with/as Elohim setting creation into time and motion.

find me is my resolution to the problematic *kanah* of buying, possessing, owning, etc. The archaic image of Yahweh acquiring this Wisdom, who is then set to work at creating, all sounds like partnership. But Yahweh is One. This sophisticated figure of Wisdom is Yahweh doing, just as the name Elohim dominates Genesis 1. This proverb seems to allude to Genesis 1, elliptically implying that Elohim is synonymous with Wisdom, playfully creating.

to brood/upon the void is my reading of the many vague translations for the movement *rakhaf* of the wind of Elohim upon the waters. The Hebrew *rakhaf* allows for the fluttering motion of a mother eagle over her clutch: *As an eagle stirs up its nest,/and hovers over its young;/as it spreads its wings, takes them up,/and bears them aloft on its pinion* (Deut 32:11): Here is Moses' comparison the Shekinah watching over Jacob. I can't resist the maternity of Wisdom brooding upon the void.

I was there is magnificently direct: creation from Wisdom.

its edges carved alludes to waves. The Tree of Life is not a tree, but all of reality: "I see Your heart in everything You've made" ("So Will I (100 Billion X)", Hillsong UNITED).

the designer is my word for a tough problem for translation. Amōn אמון only occurs here: artisan, workman, apprentice don't cut it for the hypostatic Wisdom designing creation. Artist is closer to the discovered sense of art, above pre-conceived craft, if we begin with ancient Greek art theory regarding technē. I chose designer for its functional and aesthetic connotation. Amōn, or umman swirls beautifully with amen and emunah from "Equal Arms" above.

    I feel in the various translations of Wisdom in Proverbs 8 is a playful, creative genius spontaneously co-creating and surprised by human ones when they align with their divine image and likeness.

82 | **You Explore & Know Me**—quotes Ps 139:1–6, among the most integral of all of the psalms. When psalms begin *A Psalm. Of David*, Jewish tradition teaches that David is rising into the ecstasy that, except for Psalm 88, always climaxes with the Presence.

Psalm 139 is the seventh of seven (24, 40, 68, 101, 109, 110) that begin with the phrase any of us might have overlooked: *Of David. A Psalm*. But in the Jewish tradition, this signals that David was already in the ecstasy of the Spirit, the *Shekinah*. Such psalms are directly prophetic and often non-dual.

You is a name for God—*Atah*—already cited in poems above. The directness of simple moments in prayer, meditation, and every transition all point to Godself behind ourselves, with us always.

84 | **In the Streets**—quotes Prov 1:20–24. Wisdom's persona now is a prophet indicting the socio-religious power structure for their corruption. The prophetic succession in Judaism, unique in the world for its continuity over ages, according to Abraham Heschel, is the oracle of God's conscience. There is no word in Hebrew for conscience other than heart-*lev*. The state of the heart manifests without, to which Wisdom testifies.

animals—is my translation of *petayim*, usually translated as naive or simple ones, or even fools. These English words don't bite through the innocence of the problem that is much darker. Consider White American post-war entitlement that, in its decline, looks back with nostalgia with the desire to reclaim its power. Such animal desires for dominance stem from the evil inclination, what the Jewish tradition calls the *sitra ahara* : to receive for oneself alone.

How long is a hammering anaphora that reads as interrogative and declarative.

to gather you together alludes to Yeshua's lamentation over *Jerusalem, Jerusalem, the city that kills the prophets and stones those who are sent to it! How often have I desired to gather your children together as a hen gathers her brood under her wings, and you were not willing! See, your house is left to you, desolate* (Matt 23:37–38). With this tender, maternal image, Yeshua is a mother bird. But her young refuse to gather beneath her wings. They will do to him what has been business as usual in the un-Holy Land. Its corruption within brought about its fall without in 70 CE. He is speaking from and as Wisdom.

Turn inward…distress is from Prov 8:32–34.

Return to me/& I will return to you is from Mal 3:16 merging with Yeshua's astonishing figure of himself—Wisdom—as anyone vulnerable and oppressed (Matt 25).

To you I come…you do to me—Backtrack to Luke: Yeshua has just explained to a rabbi what one must do to inherit eternal life…*to love your neighbor as yourself… But wanting to justify himself, he asked [Yeshua], 'And who is my neighbor?'* (Lk 10:27, 29). Yeshua answers with the Parable of the Good Samaritan (v. 30–37), repudiating the entire class of religious authorities, who saw Samaritans as less-than-human. To even ask this question *And who is my neighbor?* is at the same time asking, Who is human, that I'm to love them?

Back to Matt 25: Yeshua's eschatology of the judgment of the nations equates the Son of Man with a king disguised by trauma. Those at his right, saw and responded with compassion. Those at his left saw and refused: *for I was hungry and you gave me no food, I was thirsty and you gave me nothing to drink, I was a stranger and you did not welcome me, naked and you did not give me clothing, sick and in prison and you did not visit me…Truly I tell you, just as you did not do it to one of the least of these, you did not do it to me* (v. 42–43, 45). The King is not disguised at all. Our neighbor is Me: everyone through whom God breathes.

Me/Who is your conscience is from Prov 21:2: *All deeds are right in the sight of the doer,/but the Lord weighs the heart.* This exquisite image of Wisdom is echo from Egyptian mythology's Hall of Judgment. The deceased approach their own heart on a scale, weighed against the feather of Ma'at, a goddess-principle. The meanings of Ma'at concern the range from cosmic order to social justice. Ma'at was later assimilated into Isis, whose hypostasis bears the largest influence upon the Jewish conceptions of Lady Wisdom and her personification with the Shekinah, the Spirit (Schweitzer).

of inside & outside reinforces the most ancient image of scales. What's weighed is any contradiction between them. Eschatological images of God sitting in judgment hail from ancient Egypt. But Yahweh—Being—isn't judging. The contrast of God's love from what in us is unloving judges. The discrepancy between what was said and what was done judges. Conscience means heart, which I liken to a body cam: Afterlife is to watch the tape play back. Our conscience judges. This explains our cultural association of divine revelation—*apokalypsis*—with judgment as destruction. The conscience of our collective guilt and historical sin judges us.

for what is inside of you…inside of you is from Thunder: Perfect Mind 20:9–28, an ancient poem in Greek and Coptic (c. 100–230 CE) whose feminine speaker is for me the whole of nondual Wisdom. Elaine Pagels commented, "It speaks in the voice of a feminine divine power, but one that unites all opposites. One that is not only speaking in women, but also in all people" (Frontline).

While she eludes any single religious tradition, I chose to quote the rhetoric from this poem for its resonance with the persona of Lady Wisdom in Solomon's Proverbs and its foreshadow with apocryphal voices of Wisdom (see below). Wisdom is the mirror of our conscience crying out through prophets, from Amos to Malachi, who ask us where we're going. Our conscience knows. Jewish prophets reflected this conscience with sophisticated political and ecological images to wake us up. All that is happening outside reflects our own hearts inside. What we do we do to ourselves.

Me/the royal We...concludes with the refrain from Matt 25:42: *I tell you, just as you did not do it to one of the least of these, you did not do it to me.* The King is disguised by Wisdom.

88 | **All You Desire Is from You**—from Jewish mysticism of the inmost attribute of the Divine: Love, Desire, Will: *Ratzon*. Just as Yahweh is a verb and not a noun, so are all of the attributes of Yahweh, such as will, desire, arising *as a river [that] flows from Eden to water the Garden* (Gen 2:10). Yahweh is a verb, the force of all desiring within and ever beyond.

I wove you of desire—The Wisdom of Yahweh is speaking. Ours is a process of sifting false desires of our environment from true desires of our soul. The Holy Spirit, Wisdom, brokers a ceaseless negotiation of desire between our ego and our soul.

I meditate on you...to your wall flips the apocryphal voice of Sirach 14:20–25 (c 180 BCE) from a speaker meditating on Wisdom to Wisdom meditating on the reader! Feel the continuity of the voice of the Wisdom literature from Solomon to the intertestamental period. Lady Wisdom accrues even more immediacy with and as the Spirit, hunting and stalking us!

I hold your perfection…through all you desire is from *The Gospel of Truth*. A tremendous mystery that continues to astonish me: All of our true desiring and enjoyment in this life is from Yahweh as a means of returning to Yahweh. HalleluYahweh!

90 | **Is The Name of god God?**—explores a principle from Jewish mysticism of the *Shekinah*, the Holy Spirit, who is the Name—*Ha Shem*—of the Holy One. In linguistics, signs are not their signifiers, meaning everything we name only points to, but is not the phenomena of, what is named. Names and their phenomena are not the same. If this is true for ordinary nouns, how much more so the Divine?

God is spirit is from Jn 4:24. Let us hear again and again the formless verb of Spirit, with which Yeshua describes God. We lack the Hebrew name for God he would have spoken to the Samaritan woman in this Greek gospel; perhaps *Ruah*—רוח. The Greek word for God—*Theos*, θεός—will never touch the nuance of any one of the many Hebrew names for the blessed Holy One.

Spirit/one is He & His/name is She—This is equally true of the Greek for spirit—*pneuma*, πνεῦμα—which in Hebrew is an array of words synonymous with the soul as well. Principle here is the feminine Shekinah, the Indweller, the "Name" of God.

Yahweh is one/& all is one is from the Zohar (2:200a).

Elohim is the name of God throughout Gen 1. Like Yahweh, is its very complex construction eludes one gender. *El[oah] or El[a] or El[oay]* is a feminine noun for God ending with -im, a masculine plural suffix. In Jewish mysticism, Elohim is synonymous with nature and even the world, acting as the veils and process of Yahweh's revelation within and beyond.

as the name above…who comes in the name is from Ps 118:26.

where two or more are gathered is from Matt 18:20.

I am will do equates the *I am* revealed to Moses at the burning bush (Exod 3:13) with Yeshua, who speaks from the I am some ten prominent times throughout John. Lady Wisdom also speaks in Jewish scriptures as I am. Yeshua's *I am*—Εγω ειμι—sayings equate himself with and incarnate as Sophia (Scott).

the kingdom/of heaven/is feminine according to Jewish mysticism. In Hebrew, this is *Malkut*. The myriad similes and metaphors Yeshua makes of *Malkut*, the *kingdom of heaven* are all metaphors of the Holy Spirit, the Shekinah, meaning, what is manifest and knowable of the divine immanence. A precious treasure awaits one who will study all of Yeshua's figurative language of the *kingdom* as wisdom sayings of the Spirit.

in the depths…at the entrance is from Prov 8:2–3 to emphasize the immanence.

nearer to us/than we are/to ourselves is from Tau Malachi.

92 | **I Am the Breath of the Power of Elohim**—quotes from

the Wisdom of Solomon 7:25–26. This dates from around 50 BCE. Rather than Solomon speaking, I recast the speaker into the first person as Lady Wisdom herself. Feel the majesty of the wisdom literature growing across the inter-testamental period when Jewish imagination opened to Hellenistic influences. Here, Lady Wisdom is arrayed by discrete attributes, each its own profound contemplation and access to the immanent knowledge of God.

By Me… the whole world was created is from the *Zohar* (2:161a). Characteristic of this inter-testamental period of wisdom literature is the evolution of Lady Wisdom from a designer (Prov 8:30, discussed above) to Torah itself! On the surface, it's silly: the blessed Holy One reads Genesis and then creates according to it, like a cook in a kitchen following a recipe! But the Mosaic Law as we know it hadn't been revealed. What kind of Torah is this existing before creation? Astrophysical theorists are asking the same of quantum fluctuations that preexist and whose structure are evidenced from the Big Bang. Clearly, Wisdom-*Hokmah* is the subject of this teaching from the Zohar. By *Hokmah, Yahweh founded the earth…* (Prov 3:19). Equating Hokmah with Torah will later in this book foreshadow Sophia with Logos.

93 | **I Came Forth**—is a full quotation of Sirach 24:3–12. Italicizing all of this quotation, or any in this book, clogs my own versions of word and phrases, and obscures the clear, simple surface of each poem. I dare to quote whole portions of scripture to highlight underestimated moments from the Bible. I'm acting as a curator of an exhibition titled *Sophia's Wisdom*.

Here, from the mouth of *Elyon*, an inmost name of God in Jewish mysticism, Lady Wisdom is integral with the I am-*Ehyeh*. She was there in the beginning with God to create. From above the heavens, she is unknown to mortals, yet her influence pervades every human culture in its own regard for conscience (Rom 2:15).

But for Sirach, She's never fully disclosed herself to a

particular people. In her search for a resting place, Yahweh commanded and chose for Wisdom the people of Jacob to dwell: *Shekinah*, Holy Spirit, means *Indweller*. This anticipates *The Logos became flesh and dwelled-tented* (skēnoō) *among us* (Jn 1:14). In so ministering in the holy tent, Lady Wisdom becomes incarnate as Zion and Jerusalem as the center of the world. Lady Wisdom is the Presence of Yahweh in the world.

94 | **Then the Creator of All Things**—is from Song 8:5. We don't always know who the subject or object is. Is "you" the lover or the beloved? That's the power and mysticism of the Songs. The apple tree reminds us of Genesis 3, but its species is never named; Jewish tradition alleges the Tree of Knowledge was fig, based on the fig leaves later used for covering nakedness (ibid. 3:7). *Awakened* in Hebrew is ûr, a homophone for the word for the coats of *skin* Yahweh Elohim made to cover the man and woman's nakedness (ibid. v. 21). Mystical rabbis push this past the surface assumption of animal hides and posit *flesh itself*. I hear that the body is necessary for the awakening to what is beyond the body.

When you are in the light...two what will you do? is from Thomas 11. Awakening requires individuating, a painful and dangerous process in the material and spiritual life.

96 | **On Eagles' Wings I Bore You**— is from Exod 19.4. I'm extending the bearing from birth to bearing in release from slavery in Egypt. Note Yahweh's magnificent parallel of the *Shekinah* with an eagle lifting the children of Israel in their exodus.

Yet you neglected...brought you forth is from Deut 32:18. The rock that bore is *yalad* and *births* as well. Maternal connotations of this divine bearing evidence more nuanced translations of masculine-feminine balance of Yahweh. El further connotes God's great mercy and loving-kindness.

If you had walked in my way…in your sight is from Baruch 3:13–14. The book comes some five years after the fall of Jerusalem to the Babylonians (c 586 BCE). As with Sirach, Philo, and other inter-testamental writers, Lady Wisdom raises the stakes. Her address to us is a demand for inwardness, reflection, and transparency with God in others. Refusing her is to hate her; *to hate me is to love death* (Prov 8:36). More than a theological abstraction, Lady Wisdom—the Spirit—demands the whole of us in relationship. Refraining from this demand is unsustainable. Degrading people, creatures, and environments is unsustainable. Unsustainability leads to and ultimately is evil. Here is theodicy in the most organic terms.

97 | **As I Went Forth to Indwell Your Hearts**—is recast in the first person from two apocryphal sources attributed to Enoch: The Hebrew Book of Enoch 6:3 and [Ethiopian] Enoch 1 42:1–3. Both hail from around the second-century BCE. The *Hebrew Book of Enoch* was popular enough among early Christians to have been quoted by Jude (v. 14). Its appeal was for the legend—*midrash*—following the strange verse *Enoch was no more, for Elohim took him* (Gen 5:24). Whatever happened next?

The magical realism of these texts is familiar. *Enoch 1* details the corruption in the heavens above and humankind below that precipitated the collapse of the environment: the flood. People refused the teachings of Enoch, who was the voice of Wisdom in his generation. With no one to receive, *Enoch was no more, for Elohim took him* to preserve him. *Hebrew Book of Enoch* narrates Enoch's rapture into heaven. This and the other literature in his name describe his apotheosis into the supreme archangel Metatron. Compare his ascent with the departure of Lady Wisdom from the world. Like Wisdom, his absence from the world sealed its destruction. If we ignore Lady Wisdom, creation reverts to chaos.

For your crimes is from Isa 50:1. Over NRSV's *transgressions*, I prefer Daniel Matt's translation: *For your crimes, your mother was sent away* (Zohar 2:189b). *Crimes* integrates the problem of sin with life in the world. Human courts too often acquit the powerful and evil. Elohim exacts true justice in this and the afterlife by way of one's conscience. By changing this in the first-person, Wisdom repudiates hardened hearts. While this archaic language of judgment and disaster reads like it's happening to us, the Jewish mystical ethic is more concentric: The consequence is in the action: The news of any day is our collective energy on display: Conflict outside flows out of conflict unresolved inside.

98 | **Alas Alone I Sit**—is from Lam 2:11–12. Here, Lady Wisdom continues speaking, but in exile with the people. In a manner of speaking, She is divorced. This implies that the hearts of the people have turned from Yahweh: They are divorced from themselves. When She is divorced, the blessings of Yahweh go where they're not intended. Instead, they leak and spill about, empowering the Other Side: the spirits and angels of admixture and evil. This curses the people and land with oblivion.

Because there is none other than the blessed Holy One, because there is no other power, life, or force of desire other than the blessed Holy One, the problem of evil is as natural as ignorance itself. When Yeshua prayed from the cross *Father, forgive them; for they do not know what they are doing* (Lk 23:34), it's because the veils of ignorance, the uncircumcised heart, prevent knowing. This is how the Other Side manifests: through our fear, false desire, and egotism. To repent-turn from ignorance, we must learn from it. In Jewish mysticism, this is how admixture and evil play a vital role in creation. How else are we free to become conscious apart from the experience of ignorance?

99 | **Even the Jackals**—is from Lam 4:3–4. The privation of life is contrasted with jackals and ostriches, animals despised by ancient

Jews. Jeremiah's images of the starvation of children continue to sear us as people starve to this day, not from lack, but political corruption.

We are wise to find in the prophets an ethical schematic that centers justice and transparency in the conscience of the blessed Holy One within us. With Wisdom, there's life. Refusing, there's corruption as rot and decay that infect and break everything down upon its own weight.

We are clearly in the end times facing harder times to come. *Lamentations* must be read from the future as well as the past, from Jews in exile as well as us all.

Better off where those who fell...my own dead child for food is from Lam 4:9–10.

The voice of Jeremiah is the most vulnerable of the prophets. The word *jeremiad* comes from his voice. He decried the corruption of the Jewish state at every level in terms of wrenching grief. He witnessed the fall of the Temple at the hands of Babylon and died with captives in exile. His *Lamentations* is the voice of Lady Wisdom, of the *Shekinah*, in exile. This final image of oblivion is most bitter. See its precedent in 2 Kgs 6:24–30 and Deut 28:53-57. Everything said of the creative-destructive power of Wisdom in Part I has been and can manifest as desolately as the future of Cormac McCarthy's *The Road*. Jewish civilization has lived every possibility of material existence. It is from within this darkest point that the light shines, shattering the ignorance with messianic awareness.

101 | **LogoSophia**—is a concrete poem in the form of the equal-armed cross. Recall the opening poem of this book "Equal Arms." Here is a meditation on all of reality. The vertical arm represents Being: Father: Transcendent: Timeless Eternity: Heaven. The horizontal arm represents Becoming: Mother: Immanent: Time Eternity: Earth.

Here is an esoteric understanding of the Divine name Yah (Yod Heh) יה representing Yahweh as Father and Mother, respectively. Yah touches down, is manifest, with the addition of Vav He וה which represent the Bridegroom and Bride respectively. Yod Heh + Vav Heh spell the Great Name: Yahweh: יהוה. The union of the Bridegroom and Bride below manifests the union of Father and Mother above. Here invokes the great mystery of Christ the Logos and Christ the Sophia.

103 | **Before You Formed Me in Your Womb**—attempts to essentialize swathes of Greek philosophy of the Logos and Sophia into a toroidal ode of their union. Neither *Logos* nor *Sophia* translates as flatly as *Word* and *Wisdom*. I default to those flat words throughout this poem for their familiarity with readers.

    Oversimplified, Logos is nature becoming conscious of itself through all sentient beings. Discourse, ratio, proportion, intelligibility, and the interconnection of all phenomena defy a simple definition of logos. Every *-ology* of inquiry, such as bio*logy*, psycho*logy*, etc, is the expression of the Logos to itself. Further oversimplified, Wisdom is space of the Logos manifest. Wisdom is what we may know and communicate of the Logos. Wisdom is the body of the Logos. Here, let Logos be awareness and Sophia its field of display.

    Separating *LogoSophia* is as impossible as understanding what you're reading right now—Logos—without language, writing, page space and your body in this cosmos—Sophia.

    For Philo, Logos and Sophia were virtually interchangeable: "Sophia is the mother of the Logos, while [...] on the other hand, the Logos as been described as the fountain of Sophia" (Scott, 91).

    Feel with me then how far we've journeyed with *Hokmah*-Wisdom—from its inscrutability in Job, the divine co-creator and prophet woman in Proverbs, the beloved of Songs, Torah Herself in the Apocrypha—to becoming *Sophia* in the gospels. What has the Jewish *Hokmah* to do with the Greek *Sophia?* The gathering of *all people* to the blessed Holy One. Henceforth, every woman character in these poems I will name *Wisdom* for the revelation and gathering of the Word: Sophia Christology.

Mother Wisdom is based on Jer 1:4. The subject me is Mother Mary, here equated with Lady Wisdom conceiving and birthing the Word. Hear this as an ode to the Holy Spirit, Holy Wisdom.

105 | **Let It Be according to the Word**—is compressed and reshaped from Gabriel's annunciation to Mary (Lk 1:28–38). Elyon is the same Divine name associated with the Priest King Melchizedek (Gen 14:18; Ps 110:4). The nature of this breaking light is Messiah. Rather than the vertical NRSV's *overshadow you* (Lk 1:35), I chose from *episkiazō* the more concentric *envelop you.*

the Word was in the beginning links with John's prologue, which alludes as directly as it can the first three words of Genesis. Here, Wisdom is the space and speech of the Word. I build on what Meister Eckhardt once said, that every creature is a word of God, implying Wisdom's role through every act of the Word that John describes (1:1–5, 14–18).

106 | **We Have Seen Her Glory**—brings greater detail to the maternal mystery of Wisdom gestating and birthing the body of the Word.

Her Fullness, in Greek, is plērōma, another beautiful sense of the word for charis, grace.

who made known Elyon…knowing/that this is rest was grafted from the *Gospel of Truth.*

108 | **Spirit Breathing over Water**—alludes to the *Ruah Elohim* breathing over the face of the deep in Gen 1:2. *Ruah*, Spirit, Wind, is a feminine noun. Recall our discussions above Wisdom in the beginning with God. **Spirit feeding fire…**the Spirit moving makes subtle reference to the Jewish mystical teaching of elemental water, fire, and air-spirit from the *Sefer Yetzirah* (1:13): He chose three letters from among the Elementals [in the mystery of the three Mothers Alef Mem Shin (אמש)] (Kaplan, 80).

You hear Her sound…born from above is from Jn 3:3-8. We don't hear enough of the maternity of Yeshua's metaphor of the Spirit revealing our preexistence with Messiah. The poem will braid this image of maternity with baptism.

Father/in the form of the dove is from opening of Pistis Sophia (1:1:1). Pistis Sophia—*Faith Wisdom*—is a gnostic gospel of significance to Sophia Christology. It's a Coptic text of an unknown date (ranging between 200–500 CE) that narrates to the disciples the Risen Yeshua's journey and conversion of *rulers, authorities, the cosmic powers of this present darkness, the spiritual forces of evil in the heavenly places* (Eph 6:12).

The merger of the feminine Mother Spirit with the Father in the form of the dove is elegant and precise. The image flashes backward, **to Noah** (Gen 8:9,12) as a sign that the floodwaters had receded, then forward to have a place at last to rest upon **Yeshua, just as he came up/from the river.** Feel the compression of biblical time—flood to baptism—through maternal image of the dove of peace and the fulfillment of promises.

109 | **Suddenly the Spirit Tore Apart Fire Waters**—is hyper literal for the Hebrew word for heavens, *shamaim*. Their tearing apart implies the revelation of the supernal reality of the Messiah beyond the heavens entering Yeshua.

You are my Wisdom compresses divine Sonship (Mk 1:11) with Christ the *wisdom of God* (1 Cor 1:24). Hearing and receiving Messiah as the Wisdom of God acknowledges Wisdom's body-display of the Word. Christ is incarnate Wisdom (Phil 2:6–11; Col 1:15–20). Martin Scott builds on this equation of the Word with Wisdom, calling him *Jesus Sophia* (105).

well pleased to drive you leaps from Mark's *the Spirit immediately drove him out into the wilderness* (1:12) to where we left off earlier in the montage of *Lamentations*. *Wilderness* evokes the forty years of wandering during the Exodus. Wilderness also connotes desolation, exposure, and vulnerability to harsh and hostile forces. Wilderness is not literal hinterland but is also the center of any metropolis as well. Wilderness is existential exile.

110 | **Who Is She Coming Up from the Wilderness**—is a surprising play in Hebrew. Wilderness, *midbar*, holds the divine word, *d'bar*. The letter Mem in front is even the preposition *from*. Hidden in the wilderness is the Word that brings us out.

Sophia Christology reframes Christ's redemption of the world as synonymous with Sophia. The Word has come to gather in Sophia. We are Sophia. This parallels clearly with the Jewish mystical tradition of Yahweh gathering in the *Shekinah*—the *Bride*—from her exile with the people.

the kingdom, we'll recall from Jewish mysticism, is *Malkut*: the *Shekinah*, the Spirit. Not only is Yeshua teaching about the feminine Spirit through every image of the *kingdom*, he's equally speaking about how the revelation of the blessed Holy One is embodied. This is Y*our kingdom come*, not of a historical Jesus beaming up good Christians to heaven, but of the people of God embodying *Your will be done* on earth. Wisdom is the

Presence of the Word in the world.

111 | **Yeshua Said Wisdom**—is a beautiful image from Song 8:5 of the homecoming of the Shekinah from her exile. Christ the Logos is Yeshua. In my reading, shaped by my experience of the oral tradition of Tau Malachi and Tau Sarah, Christ the Sophia is inner—Mother Mary—and outer—Mary Magdalene. I have no interest in any controversies regarding the nature of their intimacy. Theologian Jean-Yves Leloup said it best in his letter requested of him from the hierarchy of the Orthodox Church: "There is no evidence that permits me to claim that Jesus expressed his full sexuality (the latter of course not reducible to genitality with Mary Magdalene or any other woman. In all respect for the strictest Orthodoxy and for the doctrine of the Incarnation, there is also no evidence that permits me to claim that he did not do so" (138). Of greater import to me is how John's prologue of the Logos unfolds his gospel of Sophia.

112 | **He Brought Me to the House of Wine**—quotes Jn 2:1–8. We know the story: Mother Mary, Yeshua, and his disciples were invited to a wedding party which ran out of wine. The context itself is life-affirming. Mother Wisdom hints at an opportunity for the Logos to be revealed publicly. Yeshua is not sure. Wisdom is sure and frames him as only a mother could:

Do whatever he tells you. As a mother bird pushing her fledgling out of the nest, he speaks instructions to the servants and the miracle of aged wine from water takes flight..

113 | **O That His Left Hand Was under My Head**— This poem continues its allusion to the return of the Bride from exile.

Now draw Her out...the juice of my pomegranates. She is the Bride, returning from her exile, as the quotation from Song 8:1–4 continues. The wine is the Bride.

The oral tradition of Tau Malachi and Tau Sarah teaches a legend that the young Magdalene was born into well-to-do family in Judea. As a spiritually prodigious child, she experienced lofty dreams and soul memories of her beloved. But her family betrothed her to a wealthy family in Babylon. En route, highwaymen raided her caravan, killed the men, and raped the women, whom they sold into sex slavery in Babylon. Her descent deepened as her astonishing beauty caught the eyes of elite men of Babylon.

Years later, having grown wealthy and influential herself, she conspired to have her captor murdered. Still, nothing could resolve the rage and despair of her soul, until the angel of Yohanan the Baptist appeared in dream. He told her that her father was dead, and that her true beloved awaited her return to the Holy Land. So this legend goes that while Mary Magdalene re-entered the gates of Jerusalem, Yeshua was performing this miracle at Cana (Malachi, 2006).

The power of legends transcends historicity, stirring familiar memories in the soul. Like any Jewish legend-*midrash* between the lines of scripture, Christian legends often say more in a simple story than can an entire book or system of theology. Of the four hermeneutical levels represented in the acronym for the "orchard" PaRDeS—*midrashim*—*D'rash*—are third next to the inmost secret—*Sod*—in the Jewish tradition. My training in these and Christian *midrashim* from Tau Malachi and Tau Sarah influence how I imagine the gospels. I will reference many more such Christian legends in later poems of this book.

114 |Before He Had Finished Speaking There Was Rebekah—quotes Eleazar's first encounter with Rebekah at the well and test for a sign of a potential wife for Isaac (Gen

24:15–18). The image of the transmission destiny at a well leaps to the next stanza:

115 | **Wisdom Said Sir You Have No Bucket**—begins a precious discourse between Yeshua and a woman of Samaria from Jn 4:7–18. We know this story also, but have not exhausted its implications for a Sophia Christology. She is Lady Wisdom scorned by religion. Yeshua's conversation with her cuts across caste lines we can't fully conceive. Whomever the majority most despises in any society, and a woman, just begins to establish this radical context.

will become in them a river bright as crystal…throne of God grafts into this imagery of the New Jerusalem (Rev 22:1) with **through Eden to water the garden** (Gen 2:10) and **gushing up out of the heart** from later in John: *'Let anyone who is thirsty come to me, and let the one who believes in me drink. As the scripture has said, "Out of the believer's heart shall flow rivers of living water"'* (Jn 7:38–39).

Tau Malachi has taught a legend behind this story that contextualizes Yeshua's calling for her husband. The surface meaning of a woman literally married and divorced five times with a sixth in the works does not explain the respect she's shown by her people: She was the first to preach the Messiah. She was a woman of Samaria, even to the surprise of Yeshua's disciples (ibid. v. 27). She is not a shamed woman. Rather, Tau Malachi has offered that she was spiritually searching, having followed many itinerant teachers who passed by this well. Her community knew her zeal and felt her word (ibid. v 39–42). I therefore translate husband *anēr* as **teacher**.

where there's no temple continues splicing into this discourse double exposures of New Jerusalem.

The Lamb of God…no need of sun or moon…its lamp/ is the Lamb I am *he, the one who is speaking to you* (Jn 4:26): This is the only direct reference in the Gospel of John of Messiah to another, a woman, of Samaria. By overlaying images of New Jerusalem within images from this discourse in John, the center of revelation focuses away from anything external to Wisdom: the heart of the voice of the one listening.

119 | **What Is the Sin of the World?**—is from the Gospel of Mary (c 100–150 CE). While much of this Gospel is fragmentary, what we have is astonishing for its depth and concision, notwithstanding its status from Mary Magdalene.

She is the subject of jealous scorn among the male disciples here and in gospels of *Philip* and *Thomas*. This chagrin continues in moments of Pistis Sophia, where she asks Yeshua the most questions and receives the most answers. Unlike the Synoptics, who all agree on Magdalene and Mary the [other] Mother [of James] as the first to witness the empty tomb, John offers the most intimate moment in all of the Christian Bible.

120 | **I Slept but My Heart Was Awake**—quotes from Song 5:2–7. We lack the space to explicate all of the moving parts in *Songs*. Lines like this one opening this stanza are packed with possibilities. How is one asleep while their heart is awake, unless the surface self is asleep, unaware of the greater depth of self?

If the reader will hold on to the Songs image of Wisdom in search of her beloved, our Sophia Christology will double expose the image of the gnostic story of *Pistis Sophia* 1:29–2:82. Faith Wisdom adores the Light of the Logos that as yet is outside of her. *Rulers, authorities, the cosmic powers of this present darkness, the spiritual forces of evil in the heavenly places* (Eph 6:12) are jealous of her potential and plot to take her light.

Making their rounds/ the guards of the gates hated me—By distracting her with false lights, to which she turns her attention and falls, they trap, strip, and rape her. She is shattered and imprisoned in the matter of this world.

Yeshua continues to narrate how Faith Wisdom cries out to the light in a cycle of thirteen repentances, each of which his disciples interpret with a psalm. Allusions to the story of Faith Wisdom will continue in the poems that follow.

those scholars/ & preachers seized me in their adultery—focuses our double exposure of Wisdom in the *Songs* and *Faith Wisdom* into the singular moment of the stoning of the adulteress (Jn 8:1–11). We know this story. But reading this through a lens of Sophia Christology expands this beyond a legal debate of orthodoxy intending to trap Yeshua to the Word gathering Wisdom from patriarchy.

Has no one condemned you? Who are our accusers but fragmented voices of deficit, separating us from our beloved? If Sophia is the display of this world-*kosmos*, just as in Jewish mysticism the Shekinah is the display of this world-*olam*, then New Testament discussions of the "world" can point to Sophia, for whom God sent the Logos. Apply this to Jn 3:16: *For God so loved Sophia.*

My claim: We are Faith Wisdom in search of the Word.

We who have ever lost ourselves, embroiled in this world of false lights and its sinful consensus, need to be awakened by the Word. This is not about the masculine rescuing the feminine. The Word is more than a man, just as Wisdom is more than a woman. The Word and Wisdom indwell us both and are the whole of ourselves as women, men, and gender-diverse people. If an outer dimension of Wisdom "sleeps," it's because of the veils necessary for individuating the Word.

forget no more— is the resolution of sin and the function of the Savior according to the quotation from the Gospel of Mary opening this poem. *I slept by my heart was awake.* To repent, to return, is to remember, awakening as from a nightmare. The inmost heart never sleeps.

When outer Wisdom comes to, wakes up, and remembers the Word indwelling all the while, the potential for the full and complete embodiment of Messiah emerges. As subsequent poems will show, the conscious union of the Word and Wisdom within us transfigures us.

125 | **The Moon Will Be like the Sun**—is from Isa 30:26. As with all of Isaiah's figurative language, Jewish mysticism derives powerful teachings from images such as these. The *Zohar* will almost always regard the moon as *Shekinah*-earth and the sun as the *Yahweh*-heaven. What does it look like when the moon shines like the sun? This is the Transfiguration of the body. When *Shekinah* and *Yahweh* embrace in conscious union, the *Shekinah* further exalts *Yahweh* in revelations of supernal grace.

flesh/is basar is literal gospel spins the two Hebrew words from their common spelling. *Good tidings* and *flesh* are the same *basar*, בשר. The implications are tremendous, radical, too simple.

Gospel is neither a book, nor limited to religious preaching. Hebrew and Greek share an etymology of their respective words for this good news from the context of war: Imagine a runner coming to us, out of breath, to tell us the enemy's been defeated! We will live! We're free! This is the deepest sense of the word *gospel*.

We hear these tidings inside, with our spirit, our heart, and our body. No two souls will hear the same gospel in the same way. The space of one is unique to that one. This is why we need more than one gospel, to capture more perspectives of salvation and liberation. If Paul has his own gospel (Rom 2:16, 16:25), then so do you and I. Our story of deliverance—*basar*—is from within and beyond our very flesh—*basar*.

come to Me quotes the familiar promise *Come to me, all you that are weary and are carrying heavy burdens, and I will give you rest. Take my yoke upon you, and learn from me; for I am gentle and humble in heart, and you will find rest for your souls. For my yoke is easy, and my burden is light* (Matt 11:28-30), but with a hyper literal reading of the word light. See the momentum of light down the page from the citation of Isaiah to Matthew as this double-exposes **from our flesh/we shall see Elohim** (Job 19:26).

126 | **Said Let There Be Light**—merges Elohim's first utterance from Gen 1:3 with Jn 1:5. The many translations of *katalambanō*—grasp, lay hold of, seize, catch, etc.—allow for many understandings of the response of the *skotia*—darkness, ignorance—to the light. We'll remember that the Jewish teaching of this light is clear, being awareness itself. Now the meaning of the hyper literal *light* of Yeshua's burden is enhanced. This light is in our body. This light IS our body but veiled by ignorance necessary for individuation. John 1:5 is conscious of what Jewish mysticism has to say about why Elohim does not call "good" the second day of creation: The division of upper from lower waters is the beginning of cosmic duality, the resurgence of primordial evil and chaos.

    The light inside this coat of skin plays with the homophone ûr for the Hebrew words for *light* אוֹר and *skin* עוֹר (Gen 3:21).

    Our **helpmate** here is not our opposite gender, but our body. The Hebrew word for helpmate doesn't translate word-for-word. Rather, a helpmate (Gen 2:18) hyper literally means *for-against*. My rhetoric in this poem claims that, regardless of our sex and gender, Eve is our life and its display.

Whoever we're with…prevents us is a play on the name Eve coded in this array of words. Eve is probably the least-understood character in all of the Bible. Apart from Jewish mystical commentary of this Jewish scripture, much of anything said about her, beginning with Paul, is either flat or offensive. I'm introducing Eve as Wisdom.

who interprets the dream of all living further plays with the name of Eve, *Havah* spelled with the same letters as the Hebrew verb *havah*, meaning to announce, tell, explain, to reveal, or display. Read hyper literally, Eve is the power of our speech. How we interpret our experience shapes what will come. Our expectations precede us.

curse of birth/is to grieve—the KJV word *sorrow* is still closer to the Hebrew word *itzabon* for the pain cursing the woman and the man, in childbearing and toil, respectively (Gen 3:16–17). My Hebrew teacher and I discussed *itzabon* at length. Pain and such still apply, but *itzabon* can also connote existential anguish. I choose the word *grieve*, for it holds the name Eve within it.

127 | **Let the Curse Be upon Me My Son**—is Rebekah's charge to Jacob, assuaging his dread of disguising himself to approach his blind father Isaac, to steal the blessing of the firstborn from his older twin brother Esau. As the matriarch, the *Shekinah* consort to Isaac, Rebekah's seen that Jacob's the rightful heir, though he's younger and less-favored than Esau (Gen 27:12). That she's willing to be cursed if the blessing of the first-born fails is a tremendous teaching of the feminine, meaning immersed in what is. Double expose this maternal involvement with Simeon's prophecy to Mother Mary:

a two-edged sword will pierce your own soul (Lk 2:35)

foreshadowing her grief at the foot of the cross.

will crown through pangs further allude to the grief of giving birth, as the mother pushes in her most painful contractions while the baby's head crowns.

of temple curtains alludes to the moment when Yeshua on the cross breathed his last and the temple curtain tore in two, from top to bottom (Matt 27:51; Mark 15:38).

for she'd become Eve personifies the Ark of the Covenant, the throne of the Yahweh's Presence, the *Shekinah*. The absence of the Ark from the second temple is, in one reading, the exposure of the emptiness of its institution. This is one reason why the Spirit rent its curtain. As Yeshua taught the Samaritan woman, true worship is not centered in an external place, but in Spirit and truth (Jn 4:23).

who took a pound of nard...not always have me is from Jn 12:3–8. This certainly reminds of an anonymous woman with the ointment performing the same devotion as recorded in Lk 7:36–50, Mk 14:3–9 and Matt 26:6–13. Apart from their respective accounts of the crucifixion, events that are told across all four gospels are few; this event is one such example. By quoting John's account, who clearly identifies this woman as Mary Magdalene, I call upon what I've already introduced of Mary Magdalene above.

& anointed Adam's head & feet opens this event as happening simultaneously on another plane: *The first man, Adam, became a living being; the last Adam became a life-giving spirit* (1 Cor 15:45). If Paul compares Yeshua to the Adam, we're left out of balance regarding the Eve. A Sophia Christology could complete this imbalance by exploring the Magdalene as the new Eve, reunited with the Yeshua, the new Adam. While Magdalene's gesture here is too complex for detailing, the devotion, intimacy, and prophecy startled the men for as many reasons as we can imagine.

128 | **But the Church Asked**—In earlier drafts of this poem, I wrote "But religion asked." Such different words for the same phenomenon of everything man-made! A close reading will see how the Church-religion equates with Judas. This could be very offensive to many Christian readers. I'm a Christian writer, indignant with the Church's association with selling out my Lord.

Adam said Leave Eve be…when she chose to descend rounds out a new layer interpreting Mary Magdalene as Eve. How she ever acquired such a costly offering cannot be answered historically. That she had it to offer opens a Christian legend Tau Malachi and Tau Sarah have shared from their oral tradition: When Mary returned to the Holy Land, she brought with her this nard from Babylon, acquired during her former life as an escort. It's a talisman of her sins and those of the world. As Sophia, she's preparing the Logos for sacrifice. In the oral tradition of Tau Malachi and Tau Sarah, Mary Magdalene is Faith Wisdom: the soul of the world.

she chose to descend quotes from *Pistis Sophia* 1:54:3 as an alternative reading of the fall of Eve. Opposite of Paul's indictment of Eve (1 Tim 2:8–15), we'll recall the gnostic character Faith Wisdom, who in her adoration of the Logos was distracted by a trap of the cosmic rulers. They preyed upon her fall, gang raped her, and stole her "Light Power." She cries out to the light in a series of repentance-songs, each of which raise her place. As anyone progressively healing from trauma, she finally comes to acknowledge her part in the disaster. By the eleventh song, she's firm and clearly confesses, "I chose to descend," after which the cosmic rulers swiftly lose their power to detain her. This signals the full release of the Word's grace from within Wisdom. What happens next will continue below.

127 | **Wisdom Raised** opens this penultimate poem. Our Sophia Christology is advancing towards the most intimate moment of the Bible. To perceive this, we'll need the deeper backstory of Gen 2 according to Jewish mysticism.

Adam is not a man. While Adam's pronouns in Gen 2 default to the masculine, the *adam* is better translated as *human*. This is not political correctness, but classical Hebrew. Also note the shift in divine names creating the adam: Elohim is to Genesis 1 what Yahweh Elohim is to Gen 2: Yahweh Elohim is called the "Complete Name," holding the entire balance of being and becoming, "Father" and "Mother," respectively. The breath of God—*nishmat*—connotes divine nature—*neshamah*—the preexistent soul in human beings that is without sin.

129 | **We Are the Adam Dreaming** —The rabbis teach a legend-midrash of the Original Adam—Adam Rishon—as androgynous: male and female joined back-to-back. See *Bereshit Rabbah* 8:1: "Rabbi Yirmeyah son of El'azar said, 'When the blessed Holy One created Adam, He created him androgynous, as is said: Male and female He created them (Gen 1:27).' Rabbi Shemu'el son of Nahmani said, 'When the blessed Holy One created Adam, He created him with two faces. Then He sawed him and gave him two backs, one on this side and one on that."

The sillier the legend, the deeper its secret. Here is the original state of desire without object, an unconscious union sinking deeper in the sleep from which it never said they woke (ibid. 2:21). All of scripture is as Adam dreaming: Messiah is its awakening, its resurrection. This is the thesis of this poem.

130 | **When Brought Before Our Opposite**—we seem to be drawn outside to what we lack within. Here, the androgynous Adam Rishon has become two, the man Adam and the woman Eve. This twoness is a dream of self and other, inside and outside, I and Thou: Its ignorance of union is the cause of all sin and "death."

Cleaved as a tree of life in two—Genesis 2 describes two trees, one of Life and the other of Knowledge (v. 9). A Jewish mystical reading will see one tree that manifests according to the one approaching. If inside and outside are divided, the Tree of Life will become a Tree of Knowledge, of opposites and all duality, leading to Death. In Hebrew, death—*mūt*—is the illusion of separation. Add the letter Alef to *mūt* and we have *emet*, *truth*. Alef represents oneness. Unity of opposites—*truth, emet*—dissolves the power of death, *mūt* from twoness. Understand, from this Hebrew nuance, that the separation of Adam and Eve precipitated the fall: the Tree of Knowledge, the serpent of desire outside, and the fruit simply sealed the state of separation.

but when we return to know—is from Paul (1 Cor 13:12). The Greek for knowledge, *gnōsis* is parallel with the Hebrew for knowledge, *da'at* that brings to union of all opposites. That *Adam knew his wife* (Gen 4:1) carries the same Hebraic denotation and most intimate connotation of enlightened knowledge with the blessed Holy One.

The inside like the outside…place of an image is Yeshua's beautiful language from Thomas 22 describing the alignment, the enlightenment, of image and likeness into one: **then we will awaken.**

131 | **Early the First Day of the Week**—Miriam is from Jn 20:1–16. We know this story. We've heard this a thousand Easters. But what surprises us if we hear this through a Sophia Christology?

Above, I said that unlike the Synoptics, who all agree on Magdalene and Mary the [other] Mother [of James] as the first to witness the empty tomb, John isolates an exchange between the Risen Savior and Mary Magdalene. To be sure, he appears briefly to the women in Matt 28:9–10, and to his disciples (ibid. v. 18–20, Lk 24:13–35, 36–49, and Mk 16:9–20), but these exchanges do not convey the intimacy that we feel as John draws us in: We are as Mary in our grief, turning to hear the Savior say our name.

If a tree falls in a forest, but no one's there to hear it, does it make a sound? If Yeshua rose from the dead, but there's no one to see him, does he speak our name? Peter and John saw nothing but his grave linens. Magdalene saw angels, then a sudden gardener, until hearing her name. She turned to complete the resurrection, the first to witness and preach the Risen Savior. If through the Word all things are made, then through Wisdom all things are fulfilled.

inside his empty chrysalis—for years in my iconography practice, the recurring motif of depicting Yeshua's resurrection as a butterfly won't relent. Perhaps it's as cheesy, even as saccharine as it gets. Then again, what other evidence against Bultmann's demythologizing the resurrection is greater than a caterpillar morphing into a butterfly? The deeper I look into their entomology, their imaginal discs that mysteriously reorganize the soupy chaos inside the chrysalis, the more certain I become that we too are winged beings inside our goo.

134 | **From Far behind the Garments of Earth & Sky**—opens a vision of the Risen Savior as a portal into the primordial. There are veiled hints of deep mysteries of Messiah in Jewish mysticism. *Adam Rishon*, the First Human introduced above, is as the body of *Adam Elyon*, the Supernal soul of God. The Soul and Body of Supernal Adam is the revelation of Messiah, whom Daniel beheld emanating from the Ancient One: *I saw one like a*

human being/coming with the clouds of heaven./And he came to the Ancient One and was presented before him (7:13).

Jewish mysticism goes even farther. The inmost aspect of the human soul preexists with God beyond creation: Primordial Adam, or *Adam Kadmon*.

To know what all of this means requires passing away, *for no one will see my face* (Exod 34:20). We've moved in scale from the witness of this cosmic cycle to the witness of all cosmic cycles simultaneously and beyond. I propose a vision of the Risen Savior as all of time, ever-receding. Such an inconceivable array is the revelation of the *Shekinah* of Messiah, the Wisdom of the Word, shining through the body of our faith in the Living Yeshua. We have faith in the soul of Messiah because of the witness of the Holy Bride, who is as the body of Messiah.

This entire mystery mirrors the layers of our soul in its process of fitful dreaming, lucid dreaming, and awakening from the dream. At every layer, without end, **We look & are/what we see.** Being *what we see* comes from the Gospel of Philip. Too many times, I've added and removed a final word, Magdalene's *Rabbouni*. It rhymes with *what we see* but that rhyme presents an aesthetic challenge I could not suppress. My hope is that you who know this story well already heard *Rabbouni* for yourself.

135 | **They Were Wept Crying**—is from a scene in the *Gospel of Mary*. Because Wisdom has received the Word, Wisdom is able to transmit the Word with the power of Pentecost (Acts 2). Pentecost is ceaseless.

Our Sophia Christology has transformed into a vehicle of the Second Coming: Wisdom is the Word being revealed through you and me in communities of sincere faith, hope, and love. If the First Coming revealed the Word of God, the Second Coming shall reveal the Wisdom of God.

136 | **We Who Praise You Bear Us Forth**—is a call and response hymn, compressing Yeshua's final discourse with his disciples (Jn 14–16): the promises of his Presence—the Shekinah—manifest with them as Wisdom. Hokmah-Wisdom has become incarnate Sophia-Wisdom in the figure of the Bride, the community, transmitting the Spirit of the Risen Savior. I've gathered these Johannine promises into the Bride, in honor of the promised Spirit. My prayer is that a Black choir director will find this hymn and make it blaze with song.

137 | **Shin ש / Mem מ /Alef א**—recall the elements of fire, water, and air-spirit, respectively of poems above discussing birth and baptism.

Hear! Shema! The Judaic invocation of Yahweh's unity: *Hear O Israel. The LORD our God. The LORD is One!* (Deut 6:4).

138 | **Mystery of Mother Influx**—transmitting the Word the power. Orthodox icons of the Pentecost celebrate Mother Wisdom (of Yeshua, who is named among those gathered in Acts 1:14), above whose head is a wheel of light and fire raying out upon the heads of the twelve. The oral tradition of Tau Malachi and Tau Sarah centers Pentecost on the Bride, who's about to become "Mother," initiating the twelve and all those gathered in one accord.

The New Eve…unconsumed is the burning bush. Calling Moses to lead the children of Israel out of Egypt, this image of burning but not consumed, is messianic. Jewish mystical tradition teaches that Yahweh intended to anoint Moses there and then as Messiah, but it was not yet. It would have to wait.

a ring of fire…with full force recalls the many visions

prophets describe, from Isaiah to the Revelation of the divine face: *When I saw him, I fell at his feet as though dead* (Rev 1:17). Those who have recounted experiences of angels to me without fear have not seen angels. If this is so, how much more the divine face!

139 | **The Light Is with Me**—are the words of the apotheosis of Faith Wisdom, *Pistis Sophia* (1:59:14) in conscious union with the Logos. Wisdom's journey of forgetting and remembering the Word is our journey inward as we integrate this remembrance into every aspect of our lives. Wilckens in the *Theological Dictionary of the New Testament* summed, "One may conclude that one and the same wisdom myth may be clearly discerned in all the Gnostic texts…Wisdom is a heavenly being who has fallen from the realm of her origin and is redeemed against from lost estate. She has also become the author of the fall of men and their redemption…one must come to see that he is identical with her. This process of knowledge is said to correspond to that of her destiny" (7:514).

My lord, you're on my head…ripe with salvation fully quotes the first Ode of Solomon (c 100 CE). It's replete with symbols of divine attributes from Jewish mysticism.

On my head describes anointing. **Your crown** represents the full force of divine will-desire. Those familiar with the Jewish mystical glyph called the Tree of Life will recognize its pattern in this ode.

Your branches are the flow of divine emanations in transmission, to which Yeshua, the *True Vine*, likens his disciples (Jn 15:1); *branches* in Hebrew—*banot*—is also the word for daughters, a point mystical rabbis equate with *tzaddikim*—realized ones.

Your crown is not dry or sterile but supple and fructifying.
Your fruits are full describes the Kingdom, the Presence

receiving and manifesting the Yahweh in the world, **& ripe with salvation**: embodiment: giving what is received. Here Kingdom and Crown-Will mirror Yeshua's prayer, *Your Kingdom come, your will be done* (Matt 6:10).

140 | **The Vortex Burst** is our final poem. Watch for images from Pentecost: *When the day of Pentecost had come, they were all together in one place. And suddenly from heaven there came a sound like the rush of a violent wind, and it filled the entire house where they were sitting. Divided tongues, as of fire, appeared among them, and a tongue rested on each of them. All of them were filled with the Holy Spirit and began to speak in other languages, as the Spirit gave them ability* (Acts 2:1–4).

See Pentecost double-exposed with concluding images from Rev 22:1–3: *Then the angel showed me the river of the water of life, bright as crystal, flowing from the throne of God and of the Lamb through the middle of the street of the city. On either side of the river is the tree of life with its twelve kinds of fruit, producing its fruit each month; and the leaves of the tree are for the healing of the nations.*

its healing leaves glad puns off *the leaves of the Tree of Life are for the healing of the nations.* These are personified by the twelve as each kind of fruit anointed by holy fire are made glad, **who grasp** the pun of their perceiving and receiving, that **She is a tree of life** *to those who lay hold of her;/those who hold her fast are called happy* (Prov 3:18). I opted for the more nuanced, epiphanic *grasp* over the NRSV's rendering of *tamak* as *hold her fast*. Inverting this verse to places emphasis of the Tree of Life, allows the final lines to merge its image from Genesis to Revelation into one body of vision of *Christ the power of God and wisdom of God* (1 Cor 1:24).

For you, dear reader, I pray that the Wisdom of the Word, the Bridegroom of the Bride, unite in your heart. Thank you for walking this far with me.

Bibliography

"APA Dictionary of Psychology." American Psychological Association. American Psychological Association. Accessed January 4, 2023. https://dictionary.apa.org/primary-process.

Barnstone, Willis, and Marvin W. Meyer. The Gnostic Bible. Boston: Shambhala, 2009.

Barnstone, Willis. The Other Bible: A Collection of Ancient, Esoteric Text from Judeo-Christian Traditions, Excluded from the Official Canon of the Old and New Testaments. San Francisco: HarperSanFrancisco, 1984.

Becker, Adam. "What Is Spacetime Really Made of?" Scientific American. Scientific American, February 1, 2022. https://www.scientificamerican.com/article/what-is-spacetime-really-made-of/.

Bibilium, About The Author Bibilium More from this Author, Bibilium More from this Author, and More from this Author. "Jesus Loves Me This I Know: The Remarkable Story behind the Beloved." bibilium.com. Bibilium, July 11, 2021. https://bibilium.com/jesus-loves-me-this-i-know-jesus-loves-me-song/.

Bruno, Giordano, Robert de Lucca, Richard J. Blackwell, Giordano Bruno, and Giordano Bruno. Cause, Principle, and Unity. Cambridge, UK: Cambridge University Press, 1998.

Byrne, Peter. "Bad Boy of Physics." Scientific American, 2013.

Drakeford, Jason. "What Is the Black Hole Information Paradox?

A Primer." Scientific American. Scientific American, August 16, 2022. https://www.scientificamerican.com/video/what-is-the-black-hole-information-paradox-a-primer/.

Druyan, Ann. Cosmos: A Spacetime Odyssey. USA: Netflix, 2014.

E., Nickelsburg George W, James C. VanderKam, and Klaus Baltzer. 1 Enoch: A Commentary on The Book of 1 Enoch. Minneapolis: Fortress, 2012.

Fohrer, G., and U. Wilckens. "Σοφία." Essay. In Theological Dictionary of the New Testament. Grand Rapids, Mich: Eerdmans, 2006.

Gutman, Yehoshua, and Y. Shechter. Midrash Be-Reshit Raba. Tel-Aviv: Hotsa'at Shoken, 1942.

Harrington, Daniel J. Wisdom Texts for Qumran. London: Routledge, 1996.

Hillsong UNITED. So Will I (100 Billion X), 2017.

Holy Bible: Containing the Old and New Testaments with the Apocryphal/Deuterocanonical Books: New Revised Standard Version. Oxford: Oxford University Press, 1995.

James, M. R. "Acts of John." Gnosis Archive. Gnostic Society Library, 2018. http://gnosis.org/library/actjohn.htm.

Kaplan, Aryeh. Sefer Yetzirah = the Book of Creation. York Beach, ME: Weiser, 1990.

Leloup, Jean-Yves. The Sacred Embrace of Jesus and Mary: The Sexual Mystery at the Heart of the Christian Tradition. Rochester, VT: Inner Traditions, 2006.

Malachi, Tau. "Vision of the Woman of Light & Radiant Golgotha." The Fellowship. Ecclesia Pistis Sophia, March 24, 2020. https://sophian.org/forum/viewtopic.php?f=3&t=3992.

———. St. Mary Magdalene: The Gnostic Tradition of the Holy Bride. Woodbury, MN: Llewellyn, 2006.

Matt, Daniel Chanan. God & the Big Bang: Discovering Harmony between Science & Spirituality. Woodstock, VT: Jewish Lights, 2016.

Matt, Daniel Chanan. The Zohar. Stanford, CA: Stanford University Press, 2016.

McReynolds, Paul R. Word Study Greek-English New Testament: A Literal, Interlinear Word Study of the Greek New Testament ; United Bible Societies' Third Corrected Edition with New Revised Standard Version, New Testament, and Word Study Concordance. Tyndale House Publishers, 1999.

Miller, Robert John. The Complete Gospels: Annotated Scholars Version. San Francisco, CA: Harper & Row, 1994.

Moskowitz, Clara. "Tangled Up in Spacetime." Scientific American, 2021.

Musser, George. "What Is Spacetime." Scientific American, 2021.

Odeberg, Hugo. 3 Enoch: Or, the Hebrew Book of Enoch. Memphis, TN: Old South Books, 2012.

Pagels, Elaine. "The Thunder, Perfect Mind." From Jesus to Christ. Frontline, 1994.

Particle Fever. USA: Amazon Prime, 2014.

Schmidt, Carl. Pistis Sophia. Leiden: E.J. Brill, 1978.

Schweitzer, Steven. "'The Egyptian Goddess Ma'at and Lady Wisdom in Proverbs 1–9: Reassessing Their Relationship.'" A Teacher for All Generations, 2012. https://doi.org/9789004224087.

Scott, Martin. *Sophia and the Johannine Jesus.* Sheffield: JSOT Press, 1992.

Sineokov. "Telescope :: Louise Glück." The Floating Library, October 3, 2009. https://thefloatinglibrary.com/2009/07/30/telescope-louise-gluck/.

Synkroniciti "Ein: No Thing (Ness)" and "We know this, right?" November 2023.

Turner, Michael. "Origin of the Universe." *Scientific American,* 2013.

Whitman, Walt. "When I Heard the Learn'd Astronomer by Walt..." Poetry Foundation. Poetry Foundation. Accessed January 4, 2023. https://www.poetryfoundation.org/poems/45479/when-i-heard-the-learnd-

Acknowledgements

My gratitude—

To the Most High, for this life and its privilege.

To Tau Malachi, Tau Sarah, and all of my companions of The Fellowship, for your love and faithfulness.

To Tau Sarah for titling this book!

To the staff poets—Richie Hoffman, Shira Erlichman, and Solmaz Sharif—and all of my brilliant peers of the 2022 Kenyon Review Writing Conference, who helped bring these words to light.

To James Najarian, Dianne Bilyak, Bevan Klassen, Alex de Reeder, Penelope Amadali, Katherine Jacobsen, Marion Sarkisian-Ramón, and Pat Yajima for reading these drafts.

To the Editors of

100 Subtexts "If not then at least believe," "Sagittarius A*," "To know as one is known" February 2023.

Agape Review "Word is Wisdom," October 2022.

Amethyst Review "Wisdom I Am," February 2023.

Compass Rose Literary Journal "stand with your feet," "because of novas," "you atah," "faith emunah," "rest your eyes" June 2023.

Inter et Inter "but nothing not even universes," "to even timespace," "call it a vessel our universe" March 2023.

Jotform "but nothing not even universes" "to even timespace" "call it a vessel our universe" January 2023.

Purple Unicorn "Et from Qubit," "the earth was chaos and void," "Wisdom Wanting" February 2023.

Synkroniciti "Ein: No Thing (Ness)" and "We know this, right?" November 2023.

Wayward Literature "Arrow of Time" May 2023.

White Enso "Black Mirror Haibun" May 2023.

The Write Launch "the moon will be like the sun," "said Let there be light," "whoever we're with wherever we are," February 2023.

Twice nominated for the 2023 Pushcart Prize, Michael Zysk, MFA, is the author of two poetry collections *Gnostic Triptych* and *Aegis of Waves* (Atmosphere Press) and co-author with Tau Malachi of *Gnosis of Guadalupe* (EPS Press, 2017). His poems, essays, and sculptures have appeared in dozens of journals in North America. He's an alumnus of the 2022 Kenyon Review Summer Conference and the 2021 Community of Writers. A veteran English teacher-activist and faith leader of a mystical Christian tradition, Michael lives to connect. Reach out @michaelzysk or mz@michaelzysk.com.

www.ingramcontent.com/pod-product-compliance
Lightning Source LLC
Chambersburg PA
CBHW050759160426
43192CB00010B/1578